# Whatever It Takes

### How a negative, sceptic became a successful property investor.

## Alasdair Cunningham

# LEGAL NOTICES

The information presented herein represents the view of the authors as of the date of publication. Because of the rate with which conditions change, the author reserves the right to alter and update his opinion based on the new conditions. This book is for informational purposes only. While every attempt has been made to verify the information provided in this book, neither the authors nor their affiliates/partners assume any responsibility for errors, inaccuracies or omissions. Any slights of people or organizations are unintentional. You should be aware of any laws which govern business transactions or other business practices in your country and state. Any reference to any person or business whether living or dead is purely coincidental.

Every effort has been made to represent this product and its potential accurately. Examples in these materials are not to be interpreted as a promise or guarantee of earnings. Earning potential is entirely dependent on the person using our product, ideas and techniques. We do not purport this as a "get rich scheme." Your level of success in attaining the results claimed in our materials depends on the time you devote to the program, ideas and techniques mentioned your finances, knowledge and various skills. Since these factors differ according to individuals, we cannot guarantee your success or income level nor are we responsible for any of your actions.

Any and all forward-looking statements here or on any of our sales material are intended to express our opinion of earnings potential. Many factors will be important in determining your actual results and no guarantees are made that you will achieve results similar to ours or anybody else's, in fact, no guarantees are made that you will achieve any results from our ideas and techniques in our material.

No part of this book may be reproduced or transmitted in any form whatsoever, electronic, or mechanical, including photocopying, recording, or by any informational storage or retrieval without the expressed written consent of the authors.

ALL RIGHTS RESERVED.

# Whatever It Takes.

*How a negative, Sceptic became a successful property investor.*

**Alasdair Cunningham**

# Would you like to follow my progress?

I know how difficult it can be to step out and take action. I have been there and came up with the same reasons and excuses you probably are. When I started out, I was fortunate to have a lot of support from my mentor and others on the same journey however I appreciate many don't have this. I will upload helpful videos and news for you to keep informed and up to date with.

- I will also offer you support, guidance and answer any questions you may have. I can help you with any stumbling blocks you're facing or even just give you a kick up the butt to take action.

- Ask any questions on the website and we will answer these for you.

## www.alasdair-cunningham.com

# TABLE OF CONTENTS

# Foreword

The fact that you are reading this book suggests that you want to make money in property. Congratulations, you are in the right place! Of all the people who desire to be rich and successful, very few make it. Why is this?

It is because they have misconceptions about property, money and success. I only have a short time, but please read carefully as I explain.

There are three things that you need to successfully invest in property: money, network and knowledge. The most overrated ingredient by far is money. Everybody thinks they need a big pot of money but most people don't have this so they just wait until they win the lottery or somebody gives them a big break. The truth is that nobody is ever going to give you a big break. The only way you are going to be successful is by building your network and expanding your knowledge.

The reason Alasdair is getting asked to speak all over the world and now write this book is because he started with very little and within months became financially free. Today his income is £30,000 per month and counting. I know this because I am his mentor and regularly ask to see his bank account for 'financial accountability'. In September 2017, Alasdair began using the little savings he had left to invest in his knowledge. He was very unsure and sceptical but the important thing is that he did it.

Since then I have not only gained an extraordinary success student, but a very good friend. Money doesn't change you but it exposes who you truly are. Since Alasdair has had money and influence his true character has been exposed. Namely, that is kind, hardworking, generous, faithful, committed, diligent, honest, courageous, loving and true. I have seen Alasdair with very little and I have seen him with much, I have dined with him in comfort and almost died with him in the River Nile. He is a great man and that is why I am proud to be in business with him and honoured to write this foreword.

You are about to learn the exact strategies that Alasdair used to achieve this and be amazed at the creative and innovative ways that you too can become a property mogul.

Samuel Leeds

# INTRODUCTION

I've spent most of my working life believing that I have to work extremely hard for my money. I'm an old school grafter, I always have been and always will be, but now I have combined that with working smarter and I now get paid considerably more. Since leaving school, I've always grafted for my money, nothing came easy, working 70/80hrs a week and only ever standing still was beginning to wear thin.

We were comfortable but still living month to month and without much savings. As I was self-employed, if I didn't work, I didn't get paid. If I was ill, I couldn't have time off as I didn't get paid. Now don't get me wrong, there are people in far worse situations than me, but I'd had enough of just doing OK when I see people all over the place killing it in business and life. I decided to do whatever it takes (legally and ethically) to put myself and my family in a position where we didn't have to stress about the bills this month, or next. I wanted to provide a great life for my family, not just a "getting by" life.

***"Screw it; let's just go for it, what's the worst thing that can happen?"***

This book is about my journey from making a decision to change to achieving financial freedom, building a successful property business which has an income of £30k per month and now employing staff.

# CHAPTER 1

## *Where did it all start?*

## £4320!!

If I wanted to keep my finance license that my business depended upon, I would need to pay this amount on behalf of this month's customers who had failed to keep up with their monthly repayments. This was the third month in a row where I had to pay off bad debtor's finance so I could continue to sell products on finance. My business relied heavily on customers sticking to their contracts and if a certain % of them failed to pay, it meant the finance provider would restrict my ability to offer finance options to the good paying customers.

This is a very frustrating position to be in considering 80% of the sales our business made were facilitated using finance options. If I closed my finance book at month end with more than 6% of bad debt, the finance company would restrict my options for the next month. Quite simply, this meant without finance options, 80% of my customer base could not buy. Not a great start to the new month.

Drastic changes were needed and needed quickly. Although the business made money, the way things were going, we were beginning to be cash poor. We had assets and stock around us but an ever-decreasing bank balance so our future was looking hard. This was due to having to facilitate bad debt.

It stops today; no more am I letting customers take me for a ride, no more am I paying their finance payments for them and then waiting months for them to pay me back. If they don't pay, then they bear the consequences, not me.

This whole situation made me question the morals and ethics of the franchises business model which I was becoming increasingly unhappy with. I had grown to hate what I was doing; going out to work was becoming more and more difficult, putting a smile on my face in front of bad customers was even harder and my patience with them was wearing very thin. I had to get out of this business and quickly. However, this was not as easy as it sounded as I had around £40k owed to me by my customers.

Not going to be as easy as I thought, so I just accepted that's the way things were and got on with it. I took a few days off, put a smile on it and ploughed on. I planned out how I would get the outstanding accounts brought under control and took the decision to sack off the bad paying customers as soon as they had paid off their accounts. I decided to give it 6 months and then reflect on the business and see how things were going. Don't get me wrong; it wasn't all bad. There were lots of benefits and advantages to the business. I enjoyed dealing with the good customers and enjoyed the trade as this is all I knew.

Since leaving school, I had worked in the garage and workshop trade and there are many great people in this trade. In this business I was traveling around a "patch" in Milton Keynes and would sell tools and various workshop related products to workshops and engineers. All businesses have good and bad, so the bad is to be expected, but the bad in this business was wearing me down very quickly and making me hate my work.

Did I really want to do this for the rest of my working life?

With Christmas looming I was looking forward to having some time off so I could stop thinking about the business or money. The break was great but short. I had refreshed and decided to go back to work with the same attitude and positivity I once had and things must get better. So, I spent the days before returning to work prepping my truck, ensuring it was well stocked, clean and full of bargains for my customers.

I hit the road and arrived at my first stop of the day, sales and payments were good, the customers loved the deals and the banter and mood was as you'd expect in a workshop. Things appeared to be on the up; maybe it was me? maybe I had been the problem? Maybe with a different attitude and mindset things may not be as bad as I'm thinking? The first week after Christmas was a great week which we sold well above our average and finished in the top 20 in the UK sales within the whole UK franchise network. Did I just need to change my downbeat opinion?

The rest of the month went pretty well sales wise and we got to the last week of the month, the week when customers finance payments were due to be paid. I expected a few non-payers due to the time of the year but what happened made me realise that this is not what I am going to be doing for much longer.

As a business, the finance department allowed a small percentage of non- paying customers, typically 3%, I took the decision over Christmas that I was no longer going to make finance payments for anyone and I didn't care about the effect on the business. I closed that month with nearly 30% unpaid finance accounts from bad debtors.

The effect of this was restrictions on my finance account meaning only customers with exceptional credit reports could purchase from me. I could still sell to all my customers, but if I wanted to offer finance, I would have to cover this myself. This would be highly risky and I open myself up to considerable financial loses if the customers don't pay. This is not something I was going to be doing.

Its late February and I am still struggling with collecting payments from customers who never paid in January and the next month end was looming. I was becoming increasingly stressed, unhappy and worried; Lisa and I are sat in our kitchen talking about what to do and between us we made the decision there and then that I believe was the best decision of my life.

### *"F\*\*\* this, there is more to life than this shit, we're done"*

It was around 9pm; I picked up my phone and called my local area manager, Lee. He was a great guy, had served in the RAF for many years and joined this business on his retirement. He knew what I was struggling with and in that call, I informed him of our decision to leave the business, he tried to change my mind, but I was having none of it. From this point on, it felt like I had been released from prison, not that I've experienced that, but you know what I mean. I felt trapped by this business, and now I'm free. The process of winding the business down started the very next day. I kept the news to myself for as long as I could so I could pull in as much cash without customers using me leaving as an excuse not to pay. I stopped selling to anyone I knew would mess around with my payments and only bought essential stock to see me through until I finished.

We're now in the middle of May; I had pretty much wound my business down, collected as much of the debt as possible and was not really working that much. By the time I had finished the business, returned stock and paid expenses I had some money saved so I could afford some time off to allow me time to think about my next move. I would go out once a week collecting from the remaining customers who still had outstanding debts and to this day I am still owed over £15k in bad debt; the chances of ever getting this are very slim.

Anyway, onwards and upwards. I have no regrets whatsoever as the business provided me a very comfortable living, a nice home and experiences I will never forget. I shoulder the blame for allowing customers to take advantage of me, in the early days I was not strict enough, I allowed the late payments which initially were not that often but soon escalated and this was my fault. I guess the lesson here is *"give someone an inch and they'll take a mile"*. Never again will customers dictate my business, income or happiness. The business is now closed and I no longer have anything to do with it. I have accepted I will never collect the outstanding debts.

Now, I am free to do what I want to do but what do I want to do?

The problem is I have always been a grafter; I've always worked long and hard to get what I wanted. Apart from an annual holiday with the family, I rarely took time off, and now I have so much time on my hands, time to do whatever I want. This sounds great I know, and it was for the first few weeks, but then reality crept in. What the hell am I going to do with my life? I'm 34 and surely this can't be it. I have no business, no job, no income and was beginning to feel very lost, I started to feel very low and down. Being *free* was not all it cracked up to be and I don't understand how people can go through their whole life without working.

I guess we all have low times and I'm nothing special. I don't deserve nor am asking for any special care or treatment. In reality, I have a great life, we have a nice home, beautiful family, no money worries yet I was feeling completely worthless. I had become a very negative, sceptical, down-beaten and depressed person. I had no interest or desire to do anything and my previous passions were now of no interest to me whatsoever. I had become a miserable, negative sceptic with no interest in socialising or anything else. I'll happily admit I was not the most enjoyable person to be around. I was becoming increasingly tired as I struggled sleeping and 3 – 4 hours a night was the norm which added to my woes. I couldn't settle as my mind was buzzing with thoughts constantly, where did I go wrong? Was it my fault? What now? What the heck was going on with me?

Lisa and I were sat in the kitchen I found myself becoming emotional while having a chat about what I was going to do with myself, this is something Lisa has not really seen before, just then my children arrived home and came into the room, this made me feel like a complete failure. I have always been the provider and rock for my family and now here I am at my kitchen table feeling worthless and like a complete failure. My daughter Isobel asked why my face was red and what's wrong with me, Lisa made up a reason and ushered her away. I can't even remember the excuse Lisa gave. I woke the next morning, Lisa and the children had left for work and school and I'm lying in bed, the hours had passed and its now lunch time now and I've been laying there since Lisa left at 8am. No reason to get out of bed. I hadn't been out of the house for a few days. I don't know why but I decided to call and make an appointment with the doctors.

I went to the appointment not actually knowing what I was going for. I'm old school and ignorantly believed that if you can't see that its broken or can't see blood, then it's not broken.

"Mr. Cunningham, room 4 please"

I took a seat and was met by a new doctor whom I never met before, he's very big guy, not fat, just built and of a similar shape to Tony Robbins, just not as tall.

"What can I help you with today? Mr Cunningham."

After a short pause

"I shifted forward on the chair where I sat and answered; I don't really know why I'm here, I'm sorry for wasting your time."

"How are you feeling?" He asked

I'm tired, very tired; I'm struggling to sleep and...

Before I knew I had completely broken down, I can't explain it; I remember being an emotional wreck. I was very embarrassed, I mean I'm a grown man and I cannot contain my emotions. I tried to tell him what had been going on; how I was feeling and I answered the questions he asked as best I could.

Who am I to be feeling down? I have no reasons to be down; I'm not homeless, I had money in the bank, a healthy family, food, heat, and a relatively normal life.

That dreaded word came out — the D word.

"Mr. Cunningham, you are experiencing a textbook case of severe depression."

What? Ignorantly, I've always thought depression meant you were a weak person. I now know what an idiot I was in thinking this way and apologise if me thinking that offends anyone.

I followed the doctor's advice and started to accept what was happening. Slowly with the right help and guidance, I started feeling better and started to regain a little purpose in my life. I needed to get out the house and find a job and Lisa's boss had been asking me if I could help him for a few months with doing commercial kitchen surveys for a new contract they'd recently won. I decided to go for this even if it was to just get me out of the house and give me a bit of structure to my week. This position meant I had to travel all over the UK to visit commercial kitchens. Lots of driving and I started to feel a little more valuable; not a skilled job but I was earning money again and slowly starting to feel like a normal person again. I was away from my family a few nights a week, which gave me plenty of time to have some alone time and I'm sure Lisa enjoyed the break!

I was out working in Wales and a program called "the week the landlords moved in" came on the BBC. The program follows tenants and their landlords and this week featured a 26-year-old multi-millionaire landlord called Samuel Leeds. He was only 26 yet he was millionaire through property by the age of 23. I was fascinated with how he achieved this, what could he have done that I couldn't have? I'm 36 as I write this and he had achieved so much more by the age of 23 than I did at 36. Did I mention he was still only 26!!

It's funny; I remember when I was watching the program thinking if I could just have an hour or two with him, he'll steer me right. Ironically 12 months on, we are now business partners, great friends and we regularly meet up for business and leisure.

Whilst watching the program I did the usual "who is this guy?" so I googled him and came across his website. This led me to read up on him and I read that in less than a month he would be holding a free 2-day seminar in Birmingham where we could meet him and learn all about him. I quickly booked two tickets for Lisa and I. I remember Lisa rolling her eyes when I told her a few days later that we were attending this guy's event to learn all about property investing. I can't say Lisa was overly keen, but as the supportive wife, she agreed to come along.

We arrived in Birmingham to be surrounded by around 100 other attendees. The doors opened too loud pumping music, people high fiving, and cheering. Lisa looked at me with the eyes that say "what the heck have you dragged me into?"

15 minutes later, Samuel was introduced onto the stage, WOW that guy knows how to hold an audience and keep them upbeat and interactive. We spent two long days learning all about his strategies and methods he has used to build his portfolio. I mean we were doing it, we were finding the deals, ringing agents, calling the letting agents to check for the demand, room prices and doing our own market research. For two days, he played full out teaching us exactly what he does as a full-time investor. I've been on events like this before, however, felt very uneasy as they generally are a massive sales fest from the moment you arrive to get you on another paid for event, so I was expecting some sort of further training to be offered which

I had no problem with. I once went on a forex training course, and they spend most of the day selling their next course, but added little value or lesson on the free course

Samuel's seminar was different; he spent from 9am to 7pm showing us, telling us and helping us and for 30 mins told us about his next intensive 3-day program. This was optional and it was not forced upon us at all. I was pleasantly surprised by this as I expected to be getting sold to all day just the same as I had previously experienced. Anyway, I didn't sign up. My inner voices were in over drive at the moment and I stupidly listened to them.

Day 2 came and it was much the same as day 1 but today was all about Hmo's, Lease options, other strategies and for me, this was the best day. At the end of the day, he offered further training to anyone who hadn't sign up on Saturday. My inner voices again kicked into gear, but to my shock Lisa, (the biggest skeptic in the room) got my wallet out, handed it to me and said "will you stop messing about and just go and do it. We've wanted to get into property for a long time and this is the best chance you'll get. I took a moment and went to find out more. I signed up and this was the best decision I or should I say Lisa has ever made.

I went on to do a further 3 days training with Samuel, but this time only 20 or so people were present. I remember even at the 3-day event I was still such a negative person, I actually arrived and then left the venue before it started as I had so many doubts, and thought there is no way this is going to work for me. I decided to go back seen as I had paid to be there and slowly over the next few days, I started to believe that this may be possible and it may be something I could do

Over the proceeding chapters I will explain my journey to becoming a full-time investor and property business owner within 3 months of Samuel's 3 day's training event. I'll keep things as they happened and explain how in 18 months, I have started a company called Better Sourced Ltd, which assists investors with finding property investments. I have secured a small property portfolio which consists of 2 HMO properties, 1 serviced accommodation unit and a further 2 serviced accommodation apartments going through the legal stages as I write this. My passive income stands around £3000 per month from my 2 HMO's and 1 SA property and I now have 2 full-time members of staff within Better Sourced Ltd. The business is doing very well with an income of around £30,000 per month and we have Investors worldwide asking for us to assist them purchase in the UK.

I truly believe that anyone with the right determination, drive and ambition can achieve what I have and more and I urge you please just go for it, ignore the skeptic in you, ignore the voices and just go for it.

Here's my journey, but first let me explain why I chose property.

# CHAPTER 2

## *Why Property?*

Why did I choose property? I mean why not stocks, shares or the new kid on the block Crypto!!! For me it's simple, I like to see my investment. I have no idea what crypto is or how it works; stocks/shares are to erratic for me, I always remember reading about stocks/shares and this phrase always stuck in my head;

*"Stocks go up via the stairs, and then jump out of the window."*

For me it had to be houses, Lisa and I have always wanted to have student houses, having seen some of the poor standard properties that they are offered. I've always thought if we could offer a high-end property, then we would always have tenants. I know some landlords stray away from students as they fear the parties and laddish behaviour, but on the flip to that, I know many landlords who would rather take students, one in particular, has let to students for 18 years with no issues that he can remember.

When you consider what the wealthiest businesses and entrepreneurs all invest in, property and land are still one of the very best investments. Take the McDonald's burger chain, we all know them for their fast food, but in reality, they are one of the wealthiest property owners in the world; Former McDonald's CFO Harry J. Sonneborn, is even quoted as saying,

*"We are not technically in the food business. We are in the real estate business. The only reason we sell fifteen-cent hamburgers is that they are the greatest producer of revenue, from which our tenants can pay us our rent."*

If you look at the top 100 wealthiest businessmen in the world, you'll see a large percentage of them gained their wealth through property investing.

For me property is the best form of investing, we live in arguably the most desirable place to live on the planet, so our net migration to the UK is in excess of 200,000. People from all over the EU and further afield flock to live here. The UK boasts of a booming jobs market, a wealth of technology, leading financial centers, big industry and a great multi cultural environment where people can thrive and live a fruitful life, so why wouldn't they choose to live here.

The big problem the country has is that we are only a tiny little island. It won't get any bigger and everybody needs a place to call home, so we have plenty of demand, but we currently lack supply. We are seeing house prices in some areas increase by 10% a year and more. Using history as a guide, you can see property prices tend to double every decade and this is why so many people become very wealthy by doing nothing, they just happened to buy their property at the right time and sit back, relax then sell when the price was right. Samuel calls these type of people "Accidental millionaires."

Wouldn't we all like a piece of that pie?

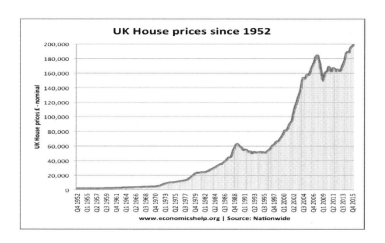

Since the 1950's, property prices have generally gone up, there are a few corrections and dips, but historically the prices have only gone one way. The good thing about property is that no matter how far back you go, the pattern is very similar. So, by gaining the knowledge and getting the correct education to ensure you're investing correctly then you give yourself the absolute best chance to profit from property.

Let's say you have £20k in savings and its sitting in a high street savings account earning approx. 0.06%, firstly whenever anything starts with 0.0... I don't get very excited. Then add into the equation that money actually decreases whilst it is in the bank then you are actually losing money. Think about it, you put £20k in the bank in 2012 and leave alone until 2017. How much do you think the £20k would be worth? The truth is it will actually be worthless. Why? Ask yourself how much cheaper was fuel in 2012 compared to 2017? I could say the same for pretty much anything, food, gas, electric. My point being as everyday objects increases in price while your £20k hasn't. It's still £20k and has become worth less. But use that same £20k wisely and invest in property and the returns are tremendous.

Here's a deal my company Better Sourced Ltd found for an investor recently. With a total investment of £17,065, my client made 23.14% return on investment. This property is in Cleethorpes and was secured for £48,500. However, the market value was actually £67,000; we secured this using our negotiations skills to get the investor a great deal. The property was in great condition and needed minimal work.

| Single Let ROI | | | |
|---|---|---|---|
| Purchase Price | 48,500.00 | | |
| Deposit | 12,125.00 | | |
| Mortgage Amount | 36,375.00 | | |
| Achievable Rent | 525.00 | | |
| | | | |
| Money In Purchase | | | |
| Deposit 25% | 12,125.00 | Monthly Costs | |
| Tax and Legals (4%) | 1,940.00 | Mortgage Payments (3%) | 90.94 |
| Renovation | 1,000.00 | Management Fee (10%) | 52.50 |
| Fee | 2,000.00 | Maintenance and Voids (10%) | 52.50 |
| Total | 17,065.00 | Utilities | 0.00 |
| | | Wifi | 0.00 |
| | | Council Tax | 0.00 |
| | | | |
| Return on Investment | | | |
| Monthly Cash flow | 329.06 | Total costs per month | 195.94 |
| Annual cash flow | 3,948.75 | | |
| | | | |
| RETURN ON INVESTMENT % | **23.14** | | |

A wise investor uses their £20k to invest in property and they stand to make nearly £20k over the 5 years. They would never achieve this return from their savings account.

The capital appreciation is variable. However, history tells us every decade property price generally double, so we estimate a £20k increase in value after 5 years. If the investor wanted to, they could refinance the property to release as much of their deposit as possible once the value is realized. They can do this because we secured the property purchase price below the true value. After a refinance, the investor can pull 75-80 % of his money out so he can invest in another property. In a lot of cases, the investors are able to pull out their full investment back.

Leverage is a wonderful tool when used in the correct way, so instead of the banks using your savings account balance to invest, you can use their money to build your portfolio. This is why I love property and for me, it had to be property. There is not to my knowledge a lender who will lend you money to buy crypto or stocks and shares. With property, you can recycle your money and grow a safe portfolio which will provide you an income indefinitely. I really don't know why everyone is not doing this.

I'll talk more about the different types of property investing in a later chapter; this book is about the exact steps which I took to become financially free from property with only a small amount of money behind me so I'll try to keep them in line with my progression.

# CHAPTER 3

*Putting yourself in the GAME!*

You must take action. That's my biggest piece of advice.
You're not going to become a property investor by sitting
on your backside thinking about it. The first thing I would
do is to educate yourself. I cannot explain how important
this is; I highly recommend Property Investors Crash
Course. This is where it all started to make sense for me.
Although I had some experience in property, I never really
understood the game until I started attending events.
There are many free events you can attend all over the
country. Please visit as many as possible before you jump
in. Education in property is essential.

I started by getting online and finding the properties that
matched my criteria, this was any property that met the
requirements for a good HMO opportunity either as an up
and running HMO or a property which needed converting.
I found 9 potential deals which I then viewed over a few
days. You can spend a fortune learning from the best in
property, but you will still be in the same place unless you
actually implement what you have been taught. For me,
it's all about action. Even if these deals are not suitable, it
doesn't matter; its all about the experience, getting out
there and meeting people in the industry.

Lots of people have a reason they can't go and view
properties but, in my opinion, if you truly want this, then
nothing should get in your way, stop letting your job,
social life, plans, excuses and negativity get in your way. I
hear too many times I work 60 hours a week; I don't have
the time to view houses; do you realise how stupid that

sounds? You're just making excuses. This is a real-life business and if you want to succeed, I've got news for you, it's not going to be easy, you're going to have to make sacrifices to get what you want and the journey is going to drive you nuts, you'll get deflated and want to give up just like I did many times. I questioned my ability more times than I care to remember. But you must believe in yourself, keep pushing and you will see results. Don't take yourself out of the game by giving up.

I didn't have a pot of cash, from memory I had less than £5k in the bank and that wouldn't be enough to buy a house as you will typically need 25% deposit, so my £5k would get me a house for £20k (not accounting for fees) I could have used that as an excuse not to view properties, but I didn't. When the agent asked me how I would be funding the purchase, I just said my house is on the market, so will be mortgaging it.

Don't let lack of funds stop you from booking viewings. It would be quite easy to say I haven't got the money, so there is no point in looking. I'll explain later why this is stupid and how I secured a low money down deal through an estate agent viewing which now makes £1400 per month income and I paid no deposit.

Some of the best deals will come your way when you're interacting the with agents. Get to know the agents; they will be your best deal finders. Over time, providing you do things correctly, you will become the go-to person for an agent when they have a deal to sell. Why? Because agents have sales targets to meet, figures to hit and commission to earn and if they can sell a deal quickly then it's good for them. The fastest way to build rapport with an agent is to buy off them, treat them with respect, turn up to appointments on time, don't mess them around and do what you said you would do. You should always treat their time like it is just as valuable as yours. Do this and believe me, they will flock to you for your business. I regularly get calls from agents I have dealt with because I am serious and someone who does what he says he is going to do.

*"Your network is your net-worth."*

Putting yourself in the game means you are building connections, getting to know people in the same industry, building a name for yourself and meeting other like-minded people. My network and connections have provided me with a list of builders, painters, electricians and plumbers and they are all from networking.

Putting myself in the game led to my first deal as a property investor even though I had less than £5k to my name. I'll explain in the next chapter how this came about.

# CHAPTER 4

## *My 1st Property Deal!*

Having invested the majority of my spare money into educating myself in property, I wasn't left with a load of money to invest, so I needed to put my training to good use. Just because I couldn't buy a property for myself didn't stop me from practicing, so I decided to put myself in the game and view properties that I found listed online that matched my criteria. I literally spent all my spare time scouring sites and looking for property and had compiled a spreadsheet with around 60 houses that matched the basic criteria for a home or multi lets. The problem was they were all over the place. I decided to focus on just one area and chose to work in Hull. Why Hull? It's a university city undergoing lots of development, it was the city of culture and benefitted from a large investment from the EU, has a thriving property market and a large employer's market. The property prices are very reasonable in Hull which adds to the appeal.

I traveled to Hull and had 9 viewings booked, eager and confident; I arrived at my first viewing at 9:15 to be met by an agent called Beth; she was lovely, very helpful and friendly but she wasn't the property expert I expected an estate agent to be. I always figured that estate agents know everything there is to know. Actually, most are sales people and have very little knowledge of property investing.

The first viewing was a group viewing, so it was a little intimidating, and I was a little nervous. I didn't want to be the amateur in the room and look stupid, so I took a look round, measured the rooms (always measure the room especially the smallest). I am yet to find the floor plan room sizes to be correct) probed the walls to check for damp, checked electrics, water and heating systems and basically just pondered about trying to look like I knew what I was doing. The property needed a lot of work and I knew it wouldn't work but trying to be a property investor and be taken seriously, I pretended to be interested. Why? I don't know really but anyways; it wasted 45 minutes of my day.

The rest of the day pretty much followed the same path as property 1. A mixture of issues in all the properties from excessive damp, subsidence are mostly just in terrible condition which deemed them of no use to me. I never managed to view all 9 I had booked and fortunately, the agents were understanding and rearranged the ones I missed for the next day. I found a hotel, got to my room and reflected on the mass of paperwork I had accumulated all day with scribbled notes and dodgy pictures and drawings.

Day 1 as a property investor left me feeling pretty deflated at this point, I felt I had spent all day viewing houses and had nothing to show for it, but I did learn some valuable lessons. Firstly, not to waste time in properties that clearly don't match your criteria and secondly be nice to estate agents. I witnessed an investor being very blunt and rude to an agent just because she wasn't sure on local rules and there's no need for it. An estate agent should be your best friend, look after them and they will return the favour. I regularly get passed off-market deals from agents I have dealt with.

Day 2 arrived and I got my first viewing at 10am, a 3bed property just off Hessle road. Pictures looked great and the price was great; only £90k for a 3bed terraced. I arrived promptly to be met by Ian, the local agent and we went inside. You know it's going to be good when they ask you to remove your shoes!! I took a look around and very quickly realised I found my first property. It had been fully refurbished top to bottom; new carpets throughout, new kitchen, bathrooms, doors and woodwork and even the electrical panel had been updated. I couldn't quite believe it; this property was perfect, the biggest problem I had was I didn't have the £22k deposit to buy it.

But there was no way I was passing on this property, so I took a few minutes in my car pretending I was doing calculations and I went back and put an offer forward, but being the cheeky investor, I am, I made an offer of £82,600. The reason being was I found a similar property on the next street sold recently for that. I used this as the reason for my offer. My mentor has always said be specific with offers and give a valid reason.

I left for my next viewing and waited eagerly for Ian to call me. The rest of the viewings that day were a waste of time, so I headed home. Around 4 pm I got a call from Ian to inform me the vendor appreciated my offer but had to reject the offer as it was too low, but he countered my offer with a nice round £85k, which was where I wanted to be from the start. I made my excuses and said I'd confirm in the morning. I had it but just wanted to delay them, so I could put the thing in place.

After speaking with my mentor, we realised that on this occasion I wasn't able to fund the deposit and with a very little network of investors, rich friends or family at this stage, I had no one that could help me on this deal. My mentor offered to help me sell it to an investor and we could split the fee. I was happy with this arrangement as I'd rather get something for it and gain the experience than have to let it go. We quickly offered this to his list of investors and to my surprise; we had several investors interested in the deal. In complete shock, we successfully sold it to an investor from London; he worked for a large banking group and was happy to pay a fee for someone to find him deals. He just didn't have the time, inclination or knowledge to find property. So, for him, a property source is ideal. I've since met the investor and he is extremely happy with this find, so much so I have now become his personal source. I know what he wants and he trusts me to find the right deals for him and he is happy paying me a hefty fee for this service. I rang the agents and told them I am happy to proceed at the £85k and I then passed the deal to the investor and he continued with the purchase.

So, my first deal, sadly I couldn't keep for myself. However, I did make money from it, I found a long-term investor with money to spend and furthermore, I gained valuable experience which would make the next property deal easier. I didn't know at this point this would be the first of many property deals and ultimately led to me opening my very own sourcing business where I deal directly with wealthy investors. It amazes me just how many opportunities are out there if you're prepared just to do it. After my first deal, I then went on to find and pass on a deal a week for 9 weeks to investors. I got paid each time and learned many lessons in the process which I'll share now

- o Treat estate agents nicely!

They will be your best property source if they like you. Do what you say you're going to do. Don't be late to appointments and be straight with them. This will go a long way. I get called a lot about off-market deals from agents because of this. Bottles of wine help also!!

- o Discipline your disappointment as my mentor is always telling me

- o There's always a way to make it happen if you want it to, just be creative.

- o I couldn't buy it, but I still profited from the deal by thinking creatively.

- o Don't waste time on properties that clearly don't fit the criteria; you should be able to walk into a house very quickly and tell if it will work or not.

My first deal was the hardest, but it gets easier; before I knew it, I had done 9 deals in 9 weeks. I couldn't afford to buy these myself, so we packaged and sold them to investors. I got a decent fee for finding the deals and was building invaluable connections with agents. These connections led to my first lease option deal which I kept for myself and here's how it came about.

# CHAPTER 5

## *It's a Keeper- My First HMO.*

Putting yourself in the game even if you may not necessarily be ready to play is a must In my opinion, Experience and opportunities will come your way. This is exactly how I came about a four bed HMO property secured using a Lease Option agreement.

On one of the viewing days, I came across this 4bed property which was perfect for multi-let conversion. It looked perfect albeit needed a light refurbishment. So, I offered on the property with the idea of selling to an investor to make a finder's fee. The property was advertised at £88,500, and my research told me that the true value was closer to £82k going by nearby sold listings; the shrewd investor in me offered £80,750 and gave my reasons for this lower offer. I also backed this up with proof of nearby sold prices in the email. I expected this to be rejected as it's a bit of a game when negotiating the price, however on this occasion, my offer was accepted very quickly, within the hour, in fact, I thought I got a bargain here.

Whilst speaking with the agents, they let on about the vendor's situation and explained that they were landlords from the south coast who purchased the house several years ago in 2007, just before the "big bang" that shook the property world. They had paid £96,500 for the property and had been letting it out on and off since. In its current state it had been vacant for 8 months. The impression I got was they were stressed landlords who didn't enjoy their time being landlords. Either way, the property should be off their hands soon enough.

A few weeks passed, I had passed the property to an investor and the sales process was now in full flow until I got a phone call from the investor to inform me that the vendors had withdrawn from the sale.

What?

Why?

It turns out they took out a 100% interest only mortgage when they bought the property in 2007 and their mortgage provider had put a stop to the sale unless the vendors could prove they could cover the mortgage shortfall. In this case, they had a shortfall of £12,000 to pay, so they needed to find approx. £12k to clear their debt with the mortgage provider. They simply could not do this, so had no choice but to pull out.

I've been taught "to discipline your disappointment!!" Easier said than done trust me, I've now got no property and a disappointed investor. I need to sort this situation out so I don't ruin my relationship with the investor. We sorted another property out for the investors which he was happy with.

A few days later I decided to try again with the property, I'm sure I could help them so I tried to find the vendors contact details so I could see if we could do something. This is not very easy especially if they don't live in the property they are selling. I rang the agents and asked for their details which obviously they were never going to give me. So, I spent a few days looking online, social media and other property listing sites and I managed to track down an old link on a letting website for the property in question, but it was from 4/5 years ago, so I didn't hold much hope of the contact box working. I sent the letting agent who was advertising the property an email asking them to pass my details to the property owners and asked them to get in touch; I never expected to hear anything more.

Several weeks later, I had forgotten about the property and I got an email from the owner of the property; they had been informed by the agent that someone was trying to get hold of them and they contacted me. They left their contact information, so I rang and introduced myself as the property investor who had previously offered on their property. I expressed a desire to purchase the deal still if we could. We had several calls and emails trying to find a suitable way of proceeding so that they don't lose money

I offered them help with letting the property out and put them in touch with some agents I knew in the area, the problem was they were having none of it, they hated being landlords. It was a dream they had several years ago and it slowly turned into a bit of a nightmare especially as they were trying to manage the tenants from the south coast which was 5hrs away. They did speak with the agent I put them in touch with but still decided they just wanted to sell up.

Because of the various issues the property was in negative equity by £12,000. They were not in a position to pay the shortfall that they would have to pay, so they are not in a great situation, I advised them that the best way forward would be to let the property out. I was starting to sound like a broken record, and they were getting a little bored of me telling them to let it out, again they insisted on not renting it out.

After another month on the market with no viewings, offers or interest from prospective buyers, I decided to offer them a more creative method of purchase. It means that they still legally own the property, but I will control it, then in a period of time, I have the opportunity to purchase at an agreed price. In the meantime, I would pay them a fee each month to cover the mortgage payments. This is known as a Lease Option purchase

They will get more money and the headache would be gone very quickly however as this is not a conventional sale, we'd need specialist solicitors to draft the legal agreements. I recommended they speak with the solicitors and have some time to think about it as they had never heard of this type of agreement so were very reluctant. A week or so later I made contact and they were keen to meet me which I was more than happy to do. I think they wanted to know if they could trust me. The meeting went well and they agreed in principle to my offer. My offer was

Purchase price in 5 years £90,500 (outstanding mortgage)

Monthly Fee £400

Their mortgage payments are £195 per month; we are over paying them by £205 per month which over the 5 years will total £12,300.

I have agreed at the time of sale; I will pay £1000 towards the seller's legal fees.

In total, they will receive

£90,500 Purchase price in 5 years

£12,300 Over payment in rent which is being paid of the mortgage each month

Total £102,800.

We will convert to an HMO at the cost of around £5000 then rent it out. The property has only recently been finished and started to get tenants paying £350 pcm per room. Total £1400 PCM, after all, costs we will make around £350 per month profit. Over the 5 years term, we will profit around £21,000 plus capital appreciation. I have a clause in the contract that allows the vendor a % of any uplift in the value at time of purchase. I'm not greedy and am fine with sharing some of the profit from the deal.

Two months later, I received the contracts and collected the keys. I now had to convert the property which involved installing fire doors, fire alarms, and a few other safety items. I planned to do this to a high spec to attract better tenants and so my property stood out. There are lots of multi-let properties out there that are just crap. They are small, cramped, poorly decorated and run down. I didn't want this, so we opted for better decoration and a homely feel throughout the property, each room has a feature wall with brand new furniture and bedding.

Here are the figures.

| | | | |
|---|---|---|---|
| **Purchase Price** | 0.00 | | |
| Deposit | 0.00 | | |
| Mortgage Amount | 0.00 | | |
| Achievable Rent | 1,400.00 | | |
| | | | |
| **Money In Purchase** | | | |
| Deposit 25% | 0.00 | **Monthly Costs** | |
| Tax and Legals (4%) | 750.00 | Mortgage Payments (3%) | 400.00 |
| Renovation | 5,000.00 | Management Fee (10%) | 168.00 |
| Finders Fee | 0.00 | Maintenance and Voids (10%) | 140.00 |
| Total | 5,750.00 | Utilities | 180.00 |
| | | Wifi | 40.00 |
| | | Council Tax | 80.00 |
| | | | |
| **Return on Investment** | | | |
| Monthly Cash flow | 392.00 | Total costs per month | 1,008.00 |
| Annual cash flow | 4,704.00 | | |
| | | | |
| **RETURN ON INVESTMENT %** | | **81.81** | |

In total, I have to pay out Legal fee's £750 plus vat and I did all conversion's and furnishing for £5000. I am making 81% Return on Investment and annual cash flow of just £4700 and this allows for voids. I'm fortunate I have my father is in the building trade so I go "family rates" for the conversions.

As part of our contract, I have the option to buy the property for a fixed price of £90.500. The property should have increased in value by then so I should also benefit from this increase. These types of investments are not for everyone; however they are great when used correctly and as long as it's a win/win for both vendor and investor they are a good thing. The vendors are now happy that they will achieve more money for their property, I cover all the expenses in the property and pay their mortgage, and they can move on with their life.

Please remember that the vendors were in a terrible situation before I helped them. They had a property in negative equity, no interested buyers, no interest in finding tenants and were losing money month after month. A lease option agreement worked well for them.

Key lessons about lease options

- It must be win/win for both parties, do not take advantage of people using this method of purchase.
- Never give up. If I gave up when the deal fell through, I would never have got the LOA
- Be open and honest at all times
- Always offer help and advice before offering an LOA

- o Don't be greedy, if the equity increases drastically, I will offer the owners a slightly higher price for the house so they can make some profit as well.

Now I had my first property in my portfolio I decided to branch out and start my very own deal packaging business, I was getting a lot of interest from investors and many requests to assist them in finding deals.

Here's how I did that.

# CHAPTER 6

## *Better Sourced Ltd, £26k in 8 weeks!*

It was around April time I decided I wanted to deal directly with investors and really get to understand the business of deal sourcing and packaging. I attended some further training and researched heavily on the business model and legal requirements to set up a deal packaging company. As an industry, the whole deal packaging and selling business appeared to be quite amateur; It seems there are lots of sourcing companies trading that quite honestly are passing deals to investors that simply do not stack up as deals. I suspect a lot of these companies are non-compliant and unregulated. What a lot of sourcing companies fail to realise is that a deal sourcing/packaging business is acting as an estate agent and as such have to meet the legal requirements of such an entity.

If I was to use the services of a deal packaging business, then I would want to know that the people I am dealing with are compliant, honest, ethical and have good business practices in place. I'd want to know that they are reputable and looking after me and my investment as they would with their own. As an investor; the first thing you should be asking any sourcing business you plan on working with is;

*"What redress scheme are you a member of and what is your membership number?"*

You should verify with the redress scheme that they are actually on the register, don't just take their word as gospel on this. Here are the questions you should be asking all deal sourcing companies before doing any business with them;

1) What property redress scheme do you belong to?

2) What is your redress scheme membership number?

3) Who provides your insurance cover and how much does this cover? Ask to see the certificate.

4) Are they registered for data protection with ICO?

5) What is their Anti Money Laundering license number?

You should be looking for the company presence online, check all social media platforms, past client reviews, check for a consistent story of the company timeline, for instance; do they keep moving addresses? Do they change names? Do they have a registered address? Are they contactable easily? Check companies house for their company name and directors? Also check the owners name under disqualified directors on companies' house.

Reputable and compliant companies should also be asking you lots of questions as part of their compliance roles, we have to carry out client due diligence, so please don't be offended if you are asked personal financial questions. You should actually be jumping for joy if they do this. This means they are doing their job correctly.

It was essential that for me to succeed in deal packaging, the first thing I had to do was set up the company, become compliant, systemise good business practices and do all this prior to passing our first deal and I suggest you do this also.

*How did I make £26k in the first 8 weeks of business?*

Until now, I had been passing the deals that I found through my mentor's business and was receiving a percentage of the fee for these deals. This was okay to start with. However, I was very aware that I'm not actually building a business here, I wanted to build my own investors database so I could sell directly. My investor's list at this point was very limited and consisted of people I'd met at various networking events and those I have spoken to online through facebook. It was a great start, but if I wanted to be successful, I needed to learn how to find investors.

Ask any marketing guru; they will all tell you the same thing,

## *"Your money is in your list."*

I now had a mission of finding investors that were looking to invest in property to join my investor's list, but not just any type of investors. I wanted hot investors that were actually looking to buy and could back up what they say up with the action. I wanted cash-rich, ready to buy, hot investors on my list, and here's how I slowly but surely started to build a very active list which grows between 40-60 new investors a week.

**Step 1** – Tell everyone what you do. Don't be ashamed or quiet about it. Shout around and ensure everyone knows.

**Step 2** – Build your online presence using Facebook, LinkedIn, Instagram and YouTube

**Step 3** – I record myself regularly and post to YouTube and Facebook letting people know what I'm viewing and what deals are coming up.

**Step 4** – Have a website created to capture leads and keep investors up to date. You may have to give something away in exchange for details, for instance, I gave away one of my basic return on Investment spreadsheets as a freebie.

**Step 5** – Network, attend as many as you can. Some of you will like this and others will hate this but get over it. Jump out of that comfort zone of yours and just do it.

**Step 6** – Immerse yourself in property

Here are my 8 Steps solution to finding investors

| | |
|---|---|
| **I** | **Identify** |
| **N** | **Network** |
| **V** | **Value** |
| **E** | **Engage** |
| **S** | **Seminars** |
| **T** | **Tell** |
| **O** | **Online** |
| **R** | **Reputation** |

**I**dentify

Firstly, you need to identify the type of investor you are looking for. There is no point in doing any marketing until you know this. At Better Sourced Ltd, we are aiming for wealthy cash-rich investors. So, we target the markets these individuals associate with.

## Network

Once you know and understand where your type of investor can be found, you need to network where they network. No point networking if your target audience are not there.

## Value

I personally would always be looking to add value to someone before trying to offer them a deal. Always offer to help someone first. This builds credibility and trust, don't be that guy who at every network event is trying to sell to every person in the room. You will quickly ruin your reputation

## Engage

Always engage with your investors. They need to hear from you regularly. Nobody builds a long-term relationship in one meeting and certainly no one hands over £1000's in finders fees to someone they have just met.

## Seminars

Attend as many seminars as possible and don't limit this to just property seminars. Wealthy investors are wealthy because they continually educate and better themselves through self-development. I get many investors from outside the property world. I attend seminars on all sorts as long as I know business minded people are going to be there.

# Tell

Tell everybody what you are doing. Use your social media profile to broadcast this. Use videos to promote your business on YouTube and other outlets.

# Online

Use online forums to add value and contribute to the any topics and forums that your potential investors use frequently. Join the forums online and add value, contribute to post, help with any questions that get asked.

# Reputation

Reputation is critical if you are to be trusted. Always do what you say you are going to do. Be nice to everyone and be an ethical and honest person at all times.

If you do all the above, your list will build. My list grows 40-60 new investors a week. The main source is through the website www.bettersourcedltd.co.uk. This is where they can join the list. The marketing I do directs them to the site, so I maintain all marketing tasks as often as possible. All of my website traffic is organic; I do not pay for any adverts online at present.

People may try and cut corners here and just buy a list of investors from a list selling service, I don't advise this. These lists are generally not that great and considering they are normally single use lists and it takes on average a potential new client 7 interactions with you to build trust; I wouldn't bother. You will also be in breach of GDPR if you use a purchased list.

**Offering your deals to your list.**

I spent the day with Samuel and he showed me how they offered the deals to their investor's list. We sent a live email to his list offering the 3 deals they had been working on that week. After we drafted the deals sheet, we hit the send button and left the office to go for lunch and by the time we got to the car, his phone started beeping. Investors were texting in to reserve the deals and requesting call backs. Within 30 mins, we had around 25 investors all wanting to reserve the 3 properties we sent out. We had lunch and headed back to the office to make the calls and speak with investors.

I couldn't believe how easy this was. Within 2 hrs of hitting the send button, we had passed on all 3 properties and the introducer's fee for each had been paid in full. All within 2 hrs! Literally, in a morning, we had passed 3 deals to investors, banked over £8000 and I just couldn't wait to get started myself. Although they made £8000 quickly, the funds were held in a client account until the property completes. You can't go on a spending spree just yet!

I had built up a small handful of investors, so the next day as I had a few deals available to offer to my investors list, I drafted an email outlining the deals I had and sent them to my list. I eagerly awaited some sort of response. 1hr passed then 2hrs passed and not one call, text or email. I spoke with Samuel to ensure I had drafted the email correctly. He assured me it was great; he told me to be patient, you've only just started. I didn't want to be patient; I wanted my phone to go crazy like I had previously seen his.

I was feeling a little deflated and thinking this wasn't going to work for me, my skepticism and negativity started to creep back in, I told you so! I thought. Who was I to think that it would work for me?

I took my dogs for a walk, so I wasn't staring at my screens waiting for them to do something. I needed to forget about things for a few hours and just chill out, so off we went for a long walk. As normal I put my earphones in and continued to listen to a video by Arnie talking about his journey to becoming The Terminator. Great video, if you get a chance you should watch it, what helped me today was the video that auto-played after Arnie's, it was called;

*"Everyone dies, but not everyone lives" by Prince Ea.*

Please watch this on YouTube. Whenever things are not going smoothly or I'm feeling low, I play this video. There are many captions in the video I continually tell myself, and I think my favourite by far is

*"Sometimes you got to leap and grow your wings on the way down."*

This quote has helped me make what should be hard decisions very easy. For instance, I was asked to speak on stage in front of 80 strangers by an event host who had followed my journey. Every part of me was saying no way, I'm not ready for that. But today I said YES and I'll just figure it out later.

Fast forward a few weeks; I'm standing in front of a crowd of people sharing a stage with Armand Morin (a very successful US internet marketing guy) who 10 years I ago, I was studying his internet marketing online training course. Now I am sharing a stage with him. WTF!! How did that happen? It's very simple I said YES! Even though I wanted to say no.

Thanks, Prince Ea. I owe you big time.

When I returned home from walking the dogs, I checked my phone and saw a missed call, this was a call from a new investor I had met at a networking meeting. His name was Adam and he was looking to buy some HMO properties and had been advised by a mortgage broker that he would unlikely secure a mortgage for an HMO as he had no landlord experience. The broker advised him first to purchase a single let property ideally below market value deal that he could add value to and then potentially release some or all of his deposit investment from the deal after the work had been done and he successfully refinanced it.

One of the deals I sent out was a 2-bed terraced property I had secured direct with the vendor as a probate sale. The family just wanted a quick sale with no hassle; we agreed a sale price of £57,000. The property was run down and tired, needed a new kitchen, bathroom, and decoration throughout. In the same street, properties were selling and had been sold recently for between £85k -£95k. We discussed the deal and I sent over the information and Adam said he would speak with his broker and let me know ASAP.

This was Adam's first investment deal; he was already a home owner so familiar with the buying processes although something that was new to Adam was not being able to view prior to paying the sourcing fee. I explained why we charge a fee, what we charge and told him all about our due diligence process, return on investment calculations and viewing process. I also reassured him on our terms and refund policies. I explained as per our terms he has a period of time to carry out all his own due diligence and if he felt the deal wasn't for him, then he could simply request a refund and walk away at no additional cost. He was fine with this and he said he'd be in touch, normally that's a polite thanks but not interested.

I headed out the following day to view some more properties; I was heading to Wolverhampton as I had a viewing booked for 11am for rent to rent prospective property. This was my first rent to rent lead, so I was pretty keen to seal this one. I arrived early, grabbed a coffee from a local costa and waited patiently in a nearby car park. I was searching online looking for other potential deals in the area that I may be able to view. As I was looking, I had a text pop up on my phone from Adam; I didn't bother opening the message just yet, I needed to be in the right frame of mind for the viewing, so the text could wait a while.

I arrived at the viewing to meet a long-term landlord called Steve, a 28yr landlord who was looking to relax a little and start to wind down his property business. I was there for around 20 mins and Steve and I spoke about my proposal for a rent to rent. His property was tired and rundown. Steve had been letting this property to students for 18 years. He was looking to get out of the game as the new rules and regs facing landlords scared him off. Steve was advertising the property as a whole house rental on gumtree. He was keen to do a deal, but we needed to agree on terms and finances. We agreed to meet up later in the week after he had some time to reflect.

As I returned to my car, I went onto my phone to use the sat-nav, so I thought I'd read Adam's text message. To my absolute shock, Adam texted me to tell me that he wanted to buy the deal we discussed yesterday. He asked me to call him to make the arrangements. I rang Adam; he confirmed he had spoken with his broker and was ready to proceed. I thanked him for trusting me and said he would have the paperwork sent over and asked him to provide us with the documents we needed to ensure we remained compliant.

I sent an email with a request for the documents we needed to carry out our due diligence on him and the source of funds, as well as our terms of business for him to review and sign if he agreed to them. We processed the paperwork and Adam was happy to proceed. The fee was paid and placed in our client account and Better Sourced Ltd had just done their first deal. I walked Adam through the process of buying the property all the way to completion. As I write this book, the tradesman are giving the property a coat of paint, new carpets and replacing the kitchen worktops and tenants are due to take the property on June 22nd paying £520pcm on a 12month term. He was advised to purchase the property on bridging finance then mortgage with a standard 75% buy to let mortgage after the refurbishment had been done. The property was valued at £90000 which allowed Adam to release a large portion of his investment. Adam spent just over £10k on the refurbishment and had to pay higher than normal lending fees for bridging finance but after the refinance he paid everyone back and was left with very little of his own money left in the deal and the property is now earning £520 pcm gross rent.

This was the first of 6 deals I passed on in the first 8 weeks which generated an income of £26,000. Better Sourced Ltd passed on 2 x Multi-let properties, 3 x Below market value deals and 1 Lease Option 5 Bed HMO property. Not bad considering I seriously doubted my abilities when it started and I didn't get any inquiries. Month after month my business grows and today employs 2 full time staff.

I sit here and its nearly Christmas, I have a healthy investor's list which is growing daily. I'm passing on several deals a week and if this continues, we are on target to hit sales of £300k in the first year. I now have investors from all over the world contacting me and I regularly have meetings with investors from all over the world to assist them. I have now employed an operations manager called Max; he deals with day to day business as well as furnishing and dressing of properties and a full-time PA who deals with all the paperwork, meetings, payments and client due diligence.

If you would like to access out deals, please feel free to join our list on our homepage of the website.

# *www.bettersourcedltd.co.uk*

My 7-step blueprint to becoming a successful deal sourcer.

| | |
|---|---|
| **S** | **Setup** |
| **O** | **Offer** |
| **U** | **Understand** |
| **R** | **Research** |
| **C** | **Clients** |
| **E** | **Exchange** |
| **R** | **Reputation** |
| **S** | **Systemise** |

# Setup

You must set your business up correctly and this involves as a minimum

- Ltd Company
- Property Redress Scheme
- Insurance
- Data Protection license
- Anti-money Laundering registration
- Website
- Marketing

# Offer

You must learn how to offer your deals to your investors list. When we offer a deal, we have investors waiting to see them and our deals are typically reserved within an hour. Mastering how you offer will make your business a whole lot easier.

# Understand

You need to understand what your investors are looking for. There is no point offering HMO's to investors only interested in BMV. Having a clear understanding of your market and investors needs mean you can market to them better.

# Research

You need to understand how to research and carry out due diligence on your investors and properties. Does the deal stack up? Would you buy it? Do the numbers work?

# Clients

Without these you will never make any money from your hard work. Master finding these and you will be able to pick and choose your clients. Sack the awkward, annoying clients and only work with the best available.

# Exchange

You need to be able to exchange to get paid, you will need contracts and paperwork in place to facilitate this.

# Reputation

Reputation is critical if you are to be trusted. Always do what you say you are going to do. Be nice to everyone and be an ethical and honest person at all times.

# Systemise

You need to systemise as much as possible within the business. Have systems in place to take care of less important roles such as CRM system for client interactions, Virtual assistants to take calls, do paperwork, finding leads, addresses etc.

## Do it right from the Start - Business Set up and Compliancy

As with any business it's very important from the very start that you set the business up correctly and are fully compliant with the law of the land you wish to operate.

You can do all this in a few hours and it's all very straight forward and simple.

Disclaimer: This is how I have set up my business after advice from my accountant and legal professionals. Please satisfy yourself that the following applies to your personal situation. Please seek advice from a legal professional and Accountant.

**Step 1.**

Set up and register your limited company.

Having a limited company set up ring fences the company's liabilities within the company and you are not personally liable. I used the formation company www.companiesmadesimple.com where you can set up your new limited company in less than 15 minutes for around £30 which includes using their addresses as your registered address.

Better Sourced Ltd is set up through this company and we used the Privacy Package which allows us to using their addresses as our registered address. Perfectly legal and if like me you work from home this will keep your home address out of the public domain. This includes a mail forwarding service for any legal documents you may receive in the post.

You can opt to use your accountant to set up your limited company however it is fairly straightforward to do and much cheaper if you do it yourself.

**Step 2.**

Insurance

You MUST be fully insured to trade Legally and you will need the following cover:

a) Professional Indemnity Insurance

Minimum cover required £100,000 to cover you for any advice which you give to an investor in a professional capacity, this insurance will also cover you for a breach of professional duty in business dealings you undertake in exchange for a fee. Please ensure you take out a suitable level of Insurance to fully cover any business dealings you undertake

b) Vehicle Insurance

If you are using a vehicle to assist with viewings then you will need to have business insurance place. It's worth keeping a vehicle record to monitor when you use the vehicle for business mileage. You may be able to just add business usage to your current insurance policy

c) Employers Liability Insurance

If applicable you will need an employer's liability policy to cover for any accidents, injuries or illness as a result of the employer's work.

My Broker is: Duncan Clark Insurance Brokers, my broker is Richard O'Neill.

01727 852299

piinsurance@dcib.co.uk

They offer a tailored Insurance package for Property Sourcing Companies.

**Step 3.**

Property Redress Scheme.

You MUST be registered with one of the following property redress schemes to be compliant and trade legally.

The Property Ombudsman

www.tpos.co.uk

Membership costs £245 plus vat

Or the Property Redress Scheme

www.theprs.co.uk

Membership Entry Level £105 plus vat

Full Membership £199 plus vat

Each of the redress Schemes have their own individual guidelines and practices who you must adhere to. Simply registering then forgetting about it is not good enough. You need to know what how each redress scheme expects you to conduct your business.

**Step 4.**

Register your company for a Data Protection License.

Visit www.ico.org.uk and register your company for a Data protection license. As you will be handling client's personal data your company must be registered. You must also ensure you handle all customer data privately and securely.

GDPR - General Data Protection Regulation

There is lots of practical tips / sites available to ensure you comply with GDPR. Please ensure you read up on this. A good book is "GDPR for Dummies"

In summary you need permission to contact people via email, if you use a well-known CRM platform such as All clients or mail chimp, they have measures in place to keep you on top of GDPR rules.

**Step 5.**

Anti-Money Laundering License

As you will be handling clients' money and receiving sums of money as payment, deposit's and reservation fee's so you will need to be registered with HMRC to minimize the risk of the funds that are being received being from criminals / terrorism for purposes of money laundering. You will need to see proof of funding source for the full purchase amount and not just your fee.

Please check HMRC Website for advice on staying compliant and learn how to keep track and monitor all your financial dealings to comply with anti-money laundering registration.

You can find out how to get registered below. You will need you UTR (Unique Tax Reference) number for your Ltd company to get registered

https://www.gov.uk/anti-money-laundering-registration

Part of the Anti-Money Laundering compliance is you as a sourcer must carry out due diligence on your clients; For instance

- o Are they who they say they are - Proof of ID - Verified by an approved professional?

- o Proof of Address

- o Proof of the source of funding

This is a legal requirement, If the client does not comply with this then simply walk away. There is a lot of guidance and help to assist with your Client Due diligence and the requirement upon your company here

https://www.gov.uk/guidance/money-laundering-regulations-your-responsibilities

Better Sourced Ltd out sources all our compliance obligations to ensure we are always compliant.

## Step 6.

Bank Accounts

You will need a business bank account. All high street banks can open this for you. I use NatWest but they all offer business banking. Be sure to open a "Client Account" at the same time.

A client account is an individual account that is used to hold funds which currently do not belong to the business, i.e.; if you're holding a deposit for a client then this money is not the businesses nor should be used to pay any business expenses. A Client account is protected should your business fail. You should store all money in the client account that is technically not yours, for instance if you have taken a fee from a client then this should be in the client account until it becomes your fee.

Costs for becoming compliant (April 2018)

| Property Sourcing Compliance Start Up Costs. | |
|---|---:|
| Set Up Limited Company | 39.99 |
| Insurance - Duncan Clark Insurance services | 350 |
| Insurance - Vehicle Business Cover added on to my personal insurance policy - I keep a mileage record | 180 |
| Property Redress - The Property Ombudsman Scheme | 294 |
| Data Protection License www.ico.org.uk | 40 |
| Anti-Money Laundering License | 240 |
| Total Start Up Costs to become Compliant | 1143.99 |

You will also need the policy and procedures, terms and conditions, risk assessments, complaints procedures and an on-going training.

Key lessons to take away from this chapter

- o Become compliant; it's not optional, its legal

  It's not difficult and will cost around £1200 and if you want to be taken seriously, this is a must

- o Build your list

- o Never give up

- o Great deals will always sell

- o Your relationship with your investor is vital, they must trust you

- o Watch "Everybody dies, but not everybody lives" by Prince EA,

# CHAPTER 7

## *HMO number 2 in the bag!*

Do you remember the rent to rent deal I was talking about? Well, Steve called me and asked me to meet him for a coffee so we could talk about the offer I had put forward. He wanted to discuss in detail the offer we made; I quizzed him a little so I knew why he wanted to give up being a landlord. He explained to me, he and his wife were actually looking to sell their property in a few years so they could retire to their holiday home abroad.

This got me thinking about my proposal, a rent to rent deal would be okay in this situation, but a lease option would be far better. This way at least we could agree to buy the property further down the line for an agreed price. We discussed using a lease option instead of a rent to rent model. I briefly explained the process and what it meant and then suggested he spoke with the solicitor so he could be sure he was comfortable with this type of set up. I am only happy to do lease options if it is the right thing for both the vendor and investor; it must be fair to both parties.

A few weeks had passed and I haven't heard from Steve. I put this down to experience, what will be will be I always say. Another day another deal. I continued with searching for deals, and had several further viewings that week when I got a text from Steve. He had spoken with the solicitor and was happy with the legalities and comfortable with me, so he would like to proceed. Great I said. I'll send you the heads of terms and we can get the ball rolling. Boom! I'd just secured my second lease option. I drafted the heads of terms which is a document to lay out the basics of the agreement which the solicitor will use to draft the legal contracts. This property was also a four-bed multi-let which is now fully tenanted and making a very healthy return.

Here is the return on investment for this property with the correct figures. The property is providing a 102% return on Investment! Wow. Who wouldn't want that deal?

I negotiated a no deposit deal as I was to carry out a refurb which included

Carpets and Vinyl floor £1200 - local contractor

Paint throughout £1000 - local contractor

Taps for kitchen and bathroom £150

Back Door £550

Tiling £350

New door handles / numbers £180

Garden clearance front and back £360

My wife, I and my dad did the rest of the work including all the cleaning. We leased the furniture pack and a HMO management company to manage the property and tenants.

| Lease Option Wolverhampton | | | |
|---|---|---|---|
| Lease payment | 500.00 | | |
| Deposit | 0.00 | | |
| Rent being achieved | 1,580.00 | Monthly Costs | |
| | | | |
| Money In Purchase | | Rent to Landlord | 500.00 |
| Refurb | 3,790.00 | Management Fee (12% of rental) | 189.60 |
| Legal Fee's | 1,042.00 | Maintenance and Voids (10% of rental) | 158.00 |
| | | Gas, Elec, Water | 95.00 |
| Total Money in | 4,832.00 | Wifi | 29.99 |
| | | Council Tax | 85.00 |
| | | TV license | 13.00 |
| | | Insurance | 18.00 |
| | | Furniture Lease | 78.00 |
| Return on Investment | | | |
| Monthly Cash flow | 413.41 | Total costs per month incl rent | 1,166.59 |
| Annual cash flow | 4,960.92 | | |
| | | | |
| RETURN ON INVESTMENT % | | **102.67** | |

Another win/win investment. Steve wanted to sell his property in a few years anyway. Now he has an agreed sale price plus he still collects rent every month until that day. I've since spoken with Steve and shown him the pictures of the refurb and he is very happy with the deal. Remember these deals must always be win/win.

# CHAPTER 8

## *Which Deal suits you?*

I get inquiries every day from those looking to start their property journey and a lot of people have no idea on the different types of property deals that they can invest in. There are many investment strategies; they all have varying barriers to entry with some needing higher cash, some needing very little cash outlay. I personally would learn to walk before you can run and would start small as I did. Before you invest in any property, please take advice from the correct people. Please do not just jump in because you're fearful of missing a deal. There are thousands of deals out there when you know how to spot them. It's really important that you first learn about each strategy before you invest in it.

Let me explain some of the different types of property investments so you can choose a path that's right for you, your budget, your experience and comfort level

### Single Lets

A single let property is a property that is let to a single family or person. You have one tenant and one Assured Short hold Tenancy agreement (AST). These are seen as the safest way of investing in property and commonly known as the least risk.

They are great for first-time investors looking for a nice return on their investment; depending on the location the monthly cash-flow may be lower than other investments. However, they are fairly safe and generally just tick along giving you a couple of hundred £ per month and growing nicely in capital appreciation. Be aware that the rents achieved and the price paid for the property is not directly related. You could buy a £300k house in the south that will rent out for £900 a month or you could get a £100k property in the Midlands that will rent out for £700 per month. Don't think because the purchase price is 3 x as much; you will achieve 3 x the rent. I would buy 3 x £100k properties instead of the £300k property as you would split your risk by a third and you'll make more cash flow per month.

**Pro's**

- Least risky strategy

- Only 1 tenant

- Easy to manage – could easily be self-managed

- Tenants pay the utility bills, council tax costs

**Con's**

- Less profit than other strategies

- If your tenant stops paying their rent, the property has no other income.

Here's an example of a single let deal I just found online.

| Single Let ROI | | | |
|---|---|---|---|
| **Purchase Price** | 71,500.00 | | |
| Deposit | 17,875.00 | | |
| Mortgage Amount | 53,625.00 | | |
| Achievable Rent | 550.00 | | |
| **Money In Purchase** | | | |
| Deposit 25% | 17,875.00 | **Monthly Costs** | |
| Tax and Legals (4%) | 2,860.00 | Mortgage Payments (3%) | 134.06 |
| Renovation | 3,000.00 | Management Fee (10%) | 55.00 |
| | | Maintenance and Voids (10%) | 55.00 |
| Total | 23,735.00 | Utilities | 0.00 |
| | | Wifi | 0.00 |
| | | Council Tax | 0.00 |
| **Return on Investment** | | | |
| Monthly Cash flow | 305.94 | Total costs per month | 244.06 |
| Annual cash flow | 3,671.25 | | |
| **RETURN ON INVESTMENT %** | | **15.47** | |

## Multi-Lets

Similar to an HMO but with fewer than 5 tenants. Typically, 4 tenants are allowed for a decent margin. Multi lets with less than 5 tenants are not required to have a license (as of Oct 2018) which means the conversion costs are considerably low. However, we always recommend that if you have a multi-let, you should install as a minimum the following safety features as a minimum and should always consult the local housing officer to seek their advice. As a general rule, we always carry out the following;

- o Fire Doors
- o Fire Alarms
- o Fire Blankets / Extinguisher
- o Signage

- o   Emergency lighting

- o   Gas and Electrical Testing Cert

You never know when the rules may change and it's better to be prepared in the event before they do. It's also good practice, as a landlord you are responsible for your tenant's safety, so installing fire safety equipment for me is a must. Please check with the local authority for their specific regulations for multi-let properties. Each authority is different and you can generally find the information online.

Here's a recent 4-bed Multi-let we sourced for a client in Burnley.

**Multi Let ROI**

| Purchase Price | 81,500.00 |
|---|---|
| Deposit | 20,375.00 |
| Mortgage Amount | 61,125.00 |
| Achievable Rent | 1,400.00 |

**Money In Purchase**

| | | **Monthly Costs** | |
|---|---|---|---|
| Deposit 25% | 20,375.00 | | |
| Tax and Legals (4%) | 3,260.00 | Mortgage Payments (3%) | 152.81 |
| Renovation | 5,500.00 | Management Fee (10%) | 168.00 |
| Finders Fee | 2,500.00 | Maintenance and Voids (10%) | 140.00 |
| Total | 31,635.00 | Utilities | 150.00 |
| | | Wifi | 40.00 |
| | | Council Tax | 80.00 |

**Return on Investment**

| | | | |
|---|---|---|---|
| Monthly Cash flow | 669.19 | Total costs per month | 730.81 |
| Annual cash flow | 8,030.25 | | |

**RETURN ON INVESTMENT %**        **25.38**

**Pro's**

- o Higher cash flow
- o Risk split by number of tenants, separate rents being paid by tenants
- o Good demand
- o Less competition than single lets

**Con's**

- o Typically, the Landlord will pay the household bills
- o Tenants tend to stay for shorter terms
- o Requires closer management
- o Household disputes between tenants
- o Higher maintenance costs
- o Higher wear and tear
- o Requires conversion to comply with regulations

**HMO**

This is a property which has a minimum of 5 tenants that are not related. As of Oct 2018, all properties that house 5 or more unrelated tenants must be licensed. The licensing is not too difficult to gain; however, you must do your homework on the local rules and regulations to ensure your property is compliant as an HMO. The fines for operating an illegal HMO are considerable.

As a licensed HMO, you will need the following as a minimum but not limited to;

- o Fire doors
- o Integrated Fire Alarm system
- o Emergency lighting
- o Emergency signage
- o Fire risk assessment
- o Electrical test certificate
- o Gas Safe certificate (if applicable)
- o Sound Proofing / Vibration testing
- o Fire Boarding
- o Minimum room sizes 6.5m2 for single use

Please check with your local authority for the exact specifications in their area. Rules vary slightly around the country and the license fees range from £600 - £1200 depending on location. It's advisable to seek advice from the HMO license dept at your local authority. I've always found them to be very helpful and for a small fee will visit your property to advise on works required before you purchase.

HMO's are a great product, as house prices and living costs increase people are increasingly looking for more affordable living costs. With an all in one fixed price for a room, HMO's provides this for the tenant. A good HMO in a good location could easily make you in excess of £1000 profit per month.

Pros and Cons are very similar to those for multi-let properties. The main difference is the cost to set up licensed HMO which will is higher than an unlicensed property due to the additional regulations for licensing

Here's a recent deal we passed to an investor. A 5-bed property in Liverpool which needed a license with a cost of £980 from the council.

**HMO ROI**

| | | | |
|---|---|---|---|
| **Purchase Price** | 88,500.00 | | |
| Deposit | 22,125.00 | | |
| Mortgage Amount | 66,375.00 | | |
| Achievable Rent | 1,700.00 | | |
| | | | |
| **Money In Purchase** | | | |
| Deposit 25% | 22,125.00 | **Monthly Costs** | |
| Tax and Legals (4%) | 3,540.00 | Mortgage Payments (3%) | 165.94 |
| Renovation | 3,500.00 | Management Fee (10%) | 204.00 |
| Finders Fee | 2,750.00 | Maintenance and Voids (10%) | 170.00 |
| License Fee | 980.00 | Utilities | 200.00 |
| Total cash in | 32,895.00 | Wifi | 40.00 |
| | | Council Tax | 85.00 |
| | | | |
| **Return on Investment** | | | |
| Monthly Cash flow | 835.06 | Total costs per month | 864.94 |
| Annual cash flow | 10,020.75 | | |
| | | | |
| **RETURN ON INVESTMENT %** | **30.46** | | |

Overall, HMO's are great investment if set up and managed correctly from the start. I would not recommend people buy an HMO property as their first investment. As with multi-let properties, always be aware of the article 4 directive when looking for potential properties.

**Rent to Rent**

As the heading says, these strategies where you find a property where the vendor allows you to rent the property under a management contract which allows you to rent the property then out. There is a management contract in place which allows you permission to then act as the property manager. Please do not confuse this with sub letting as that is illegal and should you do this strategy illegally; you could end up in serious bother.

The rent to rent strategy works well if you have a tired HMO landlord who doesn't want to or cannot sell their property as the property will have been converted. You can approach the landlord and offer them a guaranteed rent for a period of time. Rent to rent is a great way to earn money from property without actually having to buy it. I'm not the biggest fan of the rent to rent strategy as you have no option to purchase and won't acquire an asset, not necessarily a bad thing but not my preferred route.

Some people may question that if the current landlord can't make the property make money, what makes you think you can. Believe me; there are 1000's of landlords all over the country that have just had enough; they are tired of managing tenants, tired of maintenance, costs and or issues being a landlord brings. They may be in a position where they still want to keep the property, or they cannot sell the property for enough to cover their mortgage, so they are now a stressed, tired landlord.

Here's a case study of a friends rent to rent. He makes just over £500 per month from initial investment was £4000. The landlord bought the property in 2006 after several refinances, it is now due to the markets and now he is not going to make any money if he sells it, so he was happy to keep the property and allow an rent to rent.

## Rent to Rent

| | | | |
|---|---|---|---|
| Rent to Landlord | 700.00 | | |
| Deposit | 1,500.00 | | |
| Achievable Rent | 2,150.00 | **Monthly Costs** | |
| | | | |
| **Money In Purchase** | | Rent to Landlord | 700.00 |
| License Fee | 600.00 | Management Fee (12% of rental) | 258.00 |
| Furnishing | 0.00 | Maintenance and Voids (10% of rental ) | 215.00 |
| Renovation | 3,500.00 | Gas, Elec, Water | 160.00 |
| Finders Fee | 0.00 | Wifi | 40.00 |
| Deposit | 1,500.00 | Council Tax | 95.00 |
| | | TV license | 15.00 |
| Total | 5,600.00 | Insurance | 27.00 |
| | | Furniture | 108.00 |
| **Return on Investment** | | | |
| Monthly Cash flow | 532.00 | **Total costs per month incl rent** | 1,618.00 |
| Annual cash flow | 6,384.00 | Total costs excl rent | 810.00 |

**RETURN ON INVESTMENT %**       # 114.00

Rent to rent is a great way to profit from property without owning it. If you have limited funds, this may be for you. Please get suitable training before taking one on and ensure you have a legal setup company that is fully compliant to be operating an rent to rent property.

## Pro's

- o Low cash outlay.

- o Short term contract with break clauses if the investment doesn't provide good returns.

- o Low barrier to entry.

- o Great for those who cannot obtain a mortgage.

- o Great for those who cannot fund a deposit to buy.

## Con's

- o No option to buy the asset.

- o No capital appreciation.

- o Harder to secure than a conventional purchase.

## Serviced Accommodation

Serviced accommodation or apartments are much like hotels without the staff. You would offer your property either a room or the whole property out for people to book on a nightly, weekly or longer period where they can access the property and treat it like their own for as long as they are there. The host will provide a cleaning service and laundry and linen service just like in a hotel. You can find many of these on AirBnb, Booking.com, Expedia and other sites to see examples.

SA is fast becoming the new way to find accommodation on weekends away, nights out and holidays. I have colleagues and friends that prefer SA to staying in hotels as they are generally cheaper than the equivalent quality of hotels. For instance, in Cambridge city centre, you can book a 5-star reviewed SA apartment for £100 per night whereas a hotel would be in excess of £150. You can see why serviced accommodation is becoming the new trend in property investing.

**Pro's**

- o High cash flow
- o Short-term tenants
- o Huge demand
- o Room rates can be changed to suit the supply and demand very easily
- o High-profit margins
- o Very little regulation at present

**Con's**

- o Increasing competition

- o High maintenance

- o Services required such cleaners, Linen hire

- o Increased management required

**Buy Refurbish Refinance Rent**

This is a great strategy where you would find a property that needs to work. Typically, this would be a property that needs modernization to realize its true market value. These deals are everywhere, in every town and city across the country. This strategy works exceptionally well when combined with the below market value strategy which I'll talk about next.

Here's a deal an investor bought with the intentions of refurbishing, refinancing then renting it out. After all his due diligence on the property, area, demand. He has a building team in the area who quoted no more than £15k for the refurbishment which was done to a very good standard. He used bridging finance for the original purchase and then transferred this over to a buyer to let mortgage at 75% LTV rate.

**Expected**

| | |
|---|---|
| Asking price | £64,000 |
| Estimated market value | £85,000 |
| Refurbishment | £15,000 |
| Rental income | £550 pcm |

**Actual**

| | |
|---|---|
| Purchase Price | £58,000 |
| Refinanced Value | £95,000 |
| Refurbishment | £15,000 |
| Rent | £570 pcm |

The refurb took 3 months; he had a tenant lined and ready to move in straight away once the property was completed paying £570 pcm. The property was valued for lending purposes by their new mortgage lender at £95,000 which meant they could borrow 75%, £71,250. They pay the builders, bridging loan, fees and are left with only a few £1000 of their own personal funds in the deal. He can now recycle his cash and buy the next project whilst building a nice portfolio.

**Pro's**

- o Ability to refinance and release personal funds
- o Many options for financing
- o Great way to build portfolios
- o Rejuvenating run-down tired properties

**Con's**

- o Property doesn't value up correctly
- o Refurbishment can take longer than expected
- o Costs can increase if not managed properly
- o Higher fees for finance

## Below Market Value

With any property deal, we as investors are always after a bargain. If you can find any property deal that you can secure below its true market value, you are instantly in profit. It's the very best way to start off on a good investment.

There are many of these properties around and here are some reasons why a vendor may allow a BMV purchase.

- o Facing repossession
- o Probate sale
- o Separation
- o Needs refurbishment
- o Moving abroad
- o No mortgage

There are many reasons why someone would allow this type of sale. Combining a BMV purchase with any other strategy is like the icing on a cake and as an investor, you should be actively looking to get the best possible purchase price on any deal you're looking at.

Note: Please remain ethical here; it is incredibly immoral to take advantage of anyone in a bad situation just so you can get a bargain.

I find these types of deals are best sourced directly to the vendor; you'll find a lot of houses for sale online in places such as Gumtree. These vendors are typically keen to sell and more likely to take a lower offer. When I am viewing any potential deals, I listen to the vendor, find out why they are selling, and I always ask them first what is the least they will accept for the property? I am never first to offer a price. I am not there to steal their property, but let's just take this property I viewed and secured in March. It was advertised on Gumtree for a sale price of offer in the region of £85k.

The property needed around £8k-£10k spending on it and had been vacant for around 12 months. The vendor inherited the property from his parents and he just wanted it gone. There was no mortgage on the property. During the viewing, I was listening to the vendor, listening to the problems that he has had dealing with the property and trying to sell it. There had been several sales which fell through and he just wanted it out of his hair. He had listed the property at OIRO for £85k; I asked him this question and then said nothing.

*"If I can guarantee you a sale with no delays, what's the best price you will sell it for?"*

After a moment, he said if I could act quickly, no messing about and complete asap then he would take £67,500. The thing is, I would have paid more but because I kept quiet and let him tell me his best price first; we got it cheaper. We didn't take advantage of him; we didn't hard sell him, we just asked him a very simple question and let him answer. We were happy and so was he.

I accepted, shook his hand and we set about getting the purchase completed. I offered this deal to my investor's database and found him a cash buyer within 24 hrs. The property completed 6 weeks later and is now in the process of being refurbished.

There are many more routes to property success, but I would advise getting familiar with the above methods before venturing further. I believed firmly that if you want to excel in property then you need to educate yourself about the subject. Once you've mastered some of the above and have the knowledge and experience you have gained from that, then you could venture into

- o Commercial Development

- o Commercial to Residential

- o Title Splitting

- o Big Deal Lease Options

- o Castles!!! Samuel, my mentor, has just completed on a purchase of Ribbesford House, a former Castle

# CHAPTER 9

## *Third deal of the year!*

My 3rd Property of 2018

One of the things I love about having a deal packaging business is that I am always out looking at deals, an average week will see me view 20 properties and the most I viewed in one week was 52. That was a long week. I like to be out there and "keep myself in the game," and this means I'm continually building my contacts and network. I was out viewing some potential properties in Oxford and I came across this little Victorian cottage for rent. I found the lead on gumtree and I arranged to go and view the property. The property was a little run down and in the middle of being decorated. It's a quaint little place, very rustic and beautiful. It overlooks Blenheim palace and after discussing with my serviced accommodation partner and carrying out a lot of market research I was happy to proceed with this deal and a try a secure on a rent to rent basis.

I offered to rent the place for a period of 3 years and guarantee the rent if I could take the property on a management contract. He is a switched-on guy and he knows a good deal when he sees one and he quickly agreed to the deal. I took the property on an rent to rent and I planned to run it as a serviced accommodation unit with the vendor's permission.

We agreed to finish the refurb and furnish the place which we did within 2 weeks and we set the property up on a serviced accommodation management program. We had contracts drafted, agreed and signed and after a small redecoration the property went live on 21st Oct 2018 and literally within a few hours' bookings started coming in.

Here's the first week's bookings;

| | |
|---|---|
| 21st Oct | £1550 |
| 22nd Oct | £270 |
| 23rd Oct | £nil |
| 24th Oct | £1090 |
| 25th Oct | £nil |
| 26th Oct | £550 |
| 27th Oct | £1260 |

In the first week, we took £4720 in bookings all for people staying up the end of November. We have made our whole investment back in a month's worth of bookings.

November bookings came in at £3990 and December is £4210. This is a great little deal and will just tick along nicely in the background as the whole property has been systemised with cleaners, diary and management. I have very little to do with this property apart from paying the bills. After all the costs, we should be clearing around £1800 per month. We will get a clearer picture of this over the next 6 -12 months but even if the profit is less than this, we are still happy with the deal.

My passive income is close to £3000 now and things for me financially are starting to be a bit more comfortable. Better Sourced Ltd is doing very well with 2 members of staff doing the bulk of the work and my properties ticking along in the background bringing in income also. Really as I sit here writing this in mid- December. I have never been so financially secure in my life. I have a small portfolio making a nice return each month and a business making very good income. 2018 has been a year to remember.

Did I honestly think that 12 months ago I would be in this position today? No way! I've always believed one day I would but not yet or so quickly.

On New Year's Eve in 2017, I said 2018 was going to be my year and I gave it everything I've got to get there, nothing was getting in my way, I've lost friends, but made many more, I've been criticised and mocked, I've been laughed at for spending money on property education and doubted myself every day but I keep going. You only fail when you give up.

Who's laughing NOW? And what's stopping you?

# CHAPTER 10

## What Excuse are you using?

I did a poll online on various platforms whilst I was researching what people want to read about when considering investing in property. I asked them what the biggest issue stopping them following their dream of becoming a property investor was.

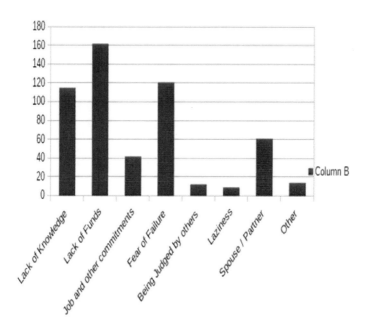

Let me show you the results 536 people who took part, all of whom were targeted due to their interest in property investing or becoming a property investor. The biggest issue was lack of funds, followed by fear of failure and lack of knowledge.

I've explained how I became an investor without having lots of money and there are loads of ways to gain knowledge. I want to talk about the two biggest things that delayed me.

**Fear of Failure**

The fear of failing is what has always stopped me really excelling in business. Because of this, I never truly put 100% into any of my previous ventures. My previous businesses were ok, I mean I made a good living out of them but they never really exploded. Why? My fear of failure stopped me from growing them; it stopped me from pushing for that big contract, it stopped me taking risks that my gut told me to take, but my mind was telling me it won't work. The thing with failure is you have to fail to win and every entrepreneur has failed at something. Failures bring very valuable lessons which make you grow in knowledge, experience, and your mind. The more you learn, the more you earn and failing will be one of the biggest learning curves you will go through.

Donald Trump; love him or hate him, has failed several times, but he is now President and a very successful businessman. Duncan Bannatyne, Lord Sugar and many others have all at some point had a business fail. They have all risen from the failures to be great successes. Look at Ray Kroc from McDonald's; he had numerous failed start-ups prior to building the McDonald's brand worldwide.

My point is get over it just like these people did, stop worrying about failing, learn as much as you can about your chosen path and just do it.

Believe me, on my journey; I've had my up and downs days when I cannot believe that my life is changing so much, days where I feel the bubble is about to burst and it's all been a dream. My life has become so busy over the last 6 months and it's non-stop which I absolutely love. I thrive when I'm busy. Please don't let irrational thoughts ruin your potential. Kick fear and doubt and tell them to do one. I've failed many times this year and every time, I grew from it. On my 121st mentoring session with Samuel, we did some goal settings for the next 12 months. These were my goals which I had 12 months to achieve.

o   1 x HMO purchase

o   1 x Lease option Property

o   Raise £30k from an investor

o   Package and sell 12 deals to investors

o   Build an Investors list of 100

o   Grow in confidence

o   Immerse myself in Property

o   Reduce my work hours and become full time in property

Samuel thought 12 months was too long, so he raised the ante and put a deadline of 31st May 2018 for me to achieve the above. We were currently in early March; my 12-month goal suddenly became my 3-month goal!

I am pleased to say I failed at this. What did I hear you say? Well, I achieved everything on the list in 3 months apart from raising £30k from an investor. But I'm pleased that I failed.

*"I would rather set my goals high and miss than set them low and hit"*

I might not have the £30k from an investor within the 3 months but I hit every other goal! plus I have grown in business, mind, knowledge, ability, confidence, heart and friends. Today I am a changed person, have a completely different mindset and outlook on everything, so please remember it's good to fail sometimes!

Incidentally I did successfully find an investor prepared to fund any deals I find as a JV. As yet I've not needed his help but that fact that I have that is great, but I'm pleased I hit succeeded in raising £30k from an investor.

## Being Judged by others

You will lose friends on your journey. Why? because most of your friends want you to fail. That's true. When they see you out shining them, jealousy kicks in. They will try to derail you on your journey. They will judge you for attending a "Property Seminar". I know people who have attended and told no one they were coming and I asked why? And their reply is that they just don't get it. Most don't get it as they are happy with a mediocre life. You and I are not and that's why we will excel.

You see lots of people will happily moan and bitch about their situation, but when it comes to the crunch, they have an opportunity to make their situation better. They simply are too lazy, risk-averse, comfortable to do anything about it. Taking the decision to become an investor means you are going to have to make sacrifices which most people are not prepared to do. People are all too happy to moan about their situation, but most lack the resolve to better themselves and do something about it.

Being judged by others was a big concern for me and I would say a big reason why I took so long to take the plunge and just do it. I didn't want to be told, "I told you it wouldn't work", or be mocked and laughed at if things went wrong. My insecurities and anxieties were going nuts at the start of my journey. I am now more determined than ever to prove these people wrong. If you have people around you dragging you down then get rid of them. If they cannot support you without question, then you don't need them in your life. You need to be around people who think like you and want to help you reach your goals. You will gain far more by having a few like-minded people in your life than having negative people around you. That's why I love networking; I attend regular networking events as the room is generally filled with people who all want to help one another, are all driven and all looking to meet people with the same drive. I've done a lot of business with contacts I met at networking events. I now host my very own network "The Property Investor's Circle". Everyone is welcomed and if you would like a free ticket to one of the events, please send me an email to info@bettersourcedltd.co.uk, and I will arrange this. Even if you are completely new, please come along, don't worry we are all very friendly and I will personally ensure you have a great evening and made to feel very welcome.

I was essentially a closet property investor in the beginning. I didn't want to tell people what I was up to and I now look back and wonder why I was like that. I know it was my fears of being judged and mocked, you see I was fighting my own confidence and anxiety battles and worried a lot about what people thought about me. This is something a lot of people suffer from and I promise you, it will not be as bad as you think it will. Now I have stepped out and told the world what I was doing I am more confident, proud and content with myself and my achievements. I did get a few passing comments from people I knew; I wouldn't call them friends just people I knew. I always remember the dig which was;

*"If this guy is that successful? why does he need to train people for money?"*

After calling him a prat! I said because Samuel's time is valuable and why should anyone expect anyone to pass on their knowledge for free? needless to say, this is the sort of comment that you hear in the pub from people who lack ambition and drive to succeed. I went onto explain that as an entrepreneur, they have multiple businesses and income streams and don't ever put all their resources in one basket.

Imagine saying to the bosses of Apple,

*"If you make so much money from selling your phones, why do you sell Mac books?"*

Only those with a poor mindset would ask such stupid questions. These are the same people that complain that the rich gets richer while the poor gets poorer. I've become very impatient towards people who are critical of those looking to do something different to what society expects of you. I've had many comments and "digs" about spending money on property education. Most from people that have racked up many thousands more in student loans to go to university, only to leave university and not even use their qualification. I mean come on get real, they'll happily spend 3-5 years at Uni, run up thousands of pounds of debt and then criticize me for investing my own money in property education instead of formal education.

# Why the Rich get Richer

### Middle Class

### Rich Mindset

| $70,000 Spent | $70,000 Invested |
|---|---|
| 15% depreciation per year: | Invested at 10% over 8 years |
| $51,000 | $66,000 |
| $43,350 | $72,600 |
| $31,320 | $87,846 |
| $26,622 | $96,631 |
| $22,629 | $106,294 |
| $19,235 | $116,923 |
| $17,349 | $128,616 |

The poor and the middle class work for money.
The rich have money work for them

I have no time for these people and have become very intolerant of them. If people are critical of me then for me it's very simple; I cut them loose. You either support my ambition or leave it's that simple. You can disagree with me and still support me which I'm fine with. The above picture speaks for itself.

# CHAPTER 11

## *What's your purpose?*

As yet I'm still struggling with my underlying purpose. My initial goals are to provide a secure home and future for my family. I want my family not to have to worry about money. So initially my goals or purpose is to provide a secure future for my family. In July, I visited Uganda on a charity trip with Samuel and some other investors. The purpose of the trip was to visit a village that Samuel had previously paid for some water tanks installed. The aim was to visit the villages and see how the village had benefitted from having fresh, clean water and then to find other villages that required water tanks and fresh water. Visiting Uganda was a life-changing experience and truly opened my eyes. Let me tell you about it.

We arrived in Entebbe; we were booked into a hotel for the first few days so we could plan our trip. Day 1 arrived and we had a team building a workshop on the beach which was run by Samuel called the "Warrior Enlightenment". The purpose of today was to learn how to deal with any problems we had previously encountered; any issue's holding us back or preventing us from following our dreams, dealing with our fears and anything else that may be preventing us from excelling. Today was all about getting rid of all the BS we use as an excuse to why things won't work. After today we have;

# "NO EXCUSES"

The following 8 days would put everything we learned from the warrior enlightenment workshop to good use. We soon realized that our problems are not problems. They mean nothing in the bigger picture. Here's us worrying about what our friends think about us and in Uganda they are worrying that they haven't eaten a proper meal in days or weeks. I actually felt a little ashamed, here we are, we live in arguably the most stable, best country in the world where we have opportunities everywhere, abundances of food and drink, work, money, welfare system, and NHS and we all take this for granted. When you witness severe poverty, kids lying on streets with nowhere to go and really no hope then believe me you will realize that the problems you are facing are really not that bad.

The first stop on our road trip was an afternoon of team building, and facing our fears. This was supposed to be a bungee jump. However, due to maintenance, the bridge was closed. So, Samuel arranged for us to go white water rafting in Jinja.

We all boarded the raft and started on the trip down the
Nile, as we drifted gently down the calm river, we were all
enjoying the scenery which was mind-blowing. Seeing the
islands and remote villages on the banks of the river were
very interesting and peaceful. Whilst in the calm waters,
our guide went through some basic safety instructions.
Firstly, he explained that the water is nothing to fear, we
all had life vests on and we will simply float if we fell in.
Just lay back and float and one of the team will be over
quickly to assist. To prove this to us and to Charles (our
Ugandan friend and guide for our whole trip) surprise the
guide on the raft. He intentionally pushed him into the
Nile, we all stopped laughing and Charles got over the
shock of being pushed into the river. Our guide showed
Charles what to do if you fall off or pushed in! I will always
remember Charles reaction to this as it was totally

unexpected and honestly one of the funniest things I have ever witnessed. Charles was pulled back onboard after being the guinea pig. Shortly after this, the guide intentionally capsized the raft, so we all had to encounter the cold water. It was actually quite funny. After the initial "ooh that's a bit cold" we had a team picture then tried our best to climb back onboard the raft which is a lot easier than it looks. All was going well with the trip. So far, it was very pleasant and enjoyable. We continued rowing for about another 20-30 minutes before we had to stop in preparation for the first waterfalls. Here we are just heading into the first set of waterfalls.

This is where we all realized that the gentle cruise, we had just experienced was about to get a whole lot more serious. Our guide gave us some last-minute instructions and we headed towards the waterfall's and rapids. Excited, nervous and exhilarated as we headed towards the falls. Here we go. HOLD ON AND GET READY!

We entered the rapids and our guide started shouting instructions "HARD LEFT" "BACK PADDLE" and various others. This is the last time I remember even having my paddle, what happened next will haunt me forever.

As we were hurtling through the first set of rapids, our raft should have been sideways going into it. However, we were actually going in with the nose. First, the front of the raft went into the plunge-pool which caused the front to lift up. I remember thinking this isn't right; the front was pointing toward the sky; the raft rolled towards the right-hand side and threw all onboard out into the water's mid rapids. I was on the left-hand side of the raft along with 4 others, so had a fair fall into the water. Myself and a few others were trapped under the raft, to this day am not sure who they were. The air pocket we were told about was not there and the raft trapped us. We were being pulled all over the place by the raft and getting dragged under the water by the currents. The raft was actually hindering us, we were getting bounced of huge rocks and it seemed it was rock and rock. I've never feared water until now and I have never felt so powerless. I kept trying to fight for air and to free myself from the raft, but felt completely powerless and just a passenger in this adventure.

Finally, I freed myself from the raft and tried my best to stay above the water, but I am now just a complete passenger in the Nile. I'm going where it takes me; I couldn't stop myself or do anything apart from trying to remain calm. After what seemed like an eternity, the waters calmed; we had made it through the waterfall and rapid to calmer waters. I was in shock; I was panicking, I was in severe pain and trying to think how the hell am I getting out of this? I had lost my helmet by this point and had thrown up due to inhaling so much water.

I was in shock and panic mode and remember shouting at myself to CALM DOWN AND THINK, the Nile appeared calm and flat but I was now drifting down the river and couldn't stop myself, I tried to swim over to the verge but couldn't. I was frantically looking for a way out and could see my friend Anna; she was in the same situation as me and about 30 feet behind me. Anna was screaming and in agony, I was trying to swim back so I could help her. This is where I realized just how powerful water is, I have never felt so powerless, trying to swim up the Nile was pointless. I was going nowhere; then I heard what sounded like more waterfalls. I turned around to take a look and I will always remember what I saw, I could see the water foaming where it went over the rocks, and I was getting pulled into this. I frantically tried to swim away from this but that was not happening, I had to accept I was going through the falls, but with no helmet, I started to panic, how deep were they? I had no idea. The guide told us to lay back, keep your legs up and hold onto to your life jacket. I was out of breath, in a lot of pain and ready to just give up. At this point, all I could think about was my family, I genuinely thought I wasn't getting out of this, I lay on my back in anticipation and I fast approached the falls. I took a deep breath and went through, I bounced straight into a cluster of rocks and remembered the sharp pain in my lower back as I landed on them, it seemed like one rock after another, then to add to that there was a whirl pool effect which kept me under water for what seemed like minutes. I actually remember thinking "This is it, I'm going to die here" I momentarily accepted this and just lay there and gave up. It was only the thoughts of my family being on their own that kept me kicking and fighting. There's no way I could do this to my wife and girls; there is no question I had to get through this.

After a few more rock encounters, I made it through the other side; I couldn't see any more waterfalls and the waters were calm. I could see Anna and swam to her. Myself and Anna spent what seemed like an age in the water waiting to be rescued by the guides. Apart from cuts and bruises, it appears Anna and I made it through in one piece. At this point, we didn't know how everyone else was.

We were picked up by the main rescue raft and they took us back up river to meet the rest of our team. Everyone was in shock and hurt in their own way with cuts and bruises. Samuel had taken the brunt of the rocks and fractured his leg; he was in a raft as he couldn't walk or bend his leg. He was bleeding terribly and had bone piercing through the skin. This was serious. We are in the middle of Africa, just north of Jinja. There is no NHS here or ambulances, we waited around an hour for a van to turn up. We then had to carry Samuel up a steep hillside while trying to support his leg to get Samuel into the van. 9 of us squeezed into this minivan and over 2 hours later we arrived at a hospital in Jinja. Samuel was in a bad way, he had lost a lot of blood and was in a lot of pain. I was in the van with Samuel's leg on my lap, so we could support his leg. His injury was bleeding heavily, although wrapped up, the blood was still coming through. We were greeted by hospital staff and they took Samuel off for treatment. We all got checked over with x-rays. As we all waited on news of Samuel, we all started to reflect on just how lucky we were.

After spending the rest of the day in the hospital getting x-rays, injections and treatment, it was clear Samuel was going nowhere. His knee needed emergency surgery and he had to stay in the hospital. Day 2 was a horrific day where I genuinely had moments where I believed I was going to die in the Nile. It sounds dramatic I know, but I assure you I had a few moments where I literally just gave up fighting and accepted what was going to happen.

At the end of the day, we were all battered, bruised and drained but we were alive. Samuel was going nowhere as he had to have emergency surgery to fix his leg. We all gathered around Samuel hospital bed and we all made a decision. Our pain was temporary, we had a job to do and we could either book into a hotel for the week and recover, or we could just continue with our mission. Samuel wouldn't have it any other way and neither would any of us. We stayed with Samuel a few hours then we all headed off in the van to a hotel for the evening. Leaving Samuel on his own in the middle of Africa with a broken leg and in a bad way was not easy, but he would have it no other way. He insisted that all of us continued with the trip.

We spent the next few days traveling by road to Kampala where we had planned to host a business workshop for locals who had a desire to start a business. We all spoke and offered help in all aspects of business to the locals. It was all very basic, but I think they really enjoyed it and found it useful. At the end of the day, we offered them the opportunity to pitch their business ideas to us like a "dragons' den" style pitch. This was great fun and everyone present filled out an application form with their business idea, set up cost and projected incomes. We read every one and selected 10 of the best to pitch their ideas to us for a chance to gain an interest-free business loan. We loaned 3 people enough money to start their businesses and we will return next year to see how this investment has gone.

The event was being promoted locally for a month prior to arriving by Charles. It was being talked about on the local radio station and many people knew about it. The event was to run from 10am to 4pm, we arrived early and set up ready to welcome the guests and give them as much help and information as we could for the short time we were there. Unfortunately, we didn't factor in the "Africa" time into our schedule. Africa time essentially means nobody arrives on time, it's normal or accepted to arrive late. So, at 10am, we had 1 person in the room. A young well-dressed lady who clearly made an effort to dress for the occasion and also turn up on time. Annoyingly the rest of the delegates didn't turn up until around 11:30!! I kicked the event off and the rest of the day went well.

Pic -Myself and Stuart Brown delivering a talk on basic money management

John Raybould, a good friend and fellow investor, was presenting his talk about time keeping and about how important it is if you want to be taken seriously. I'm sure this fell on deaf ears, but John did his best. We've had contact since with some of the delegates since our return and they really enjoyed it and felt they had to thank us for all our help. Hopefully when we return next year, the money we invested will have been well spent and making them a good return.

We now headed down to Kabale where we're going to visit Charles' home village. We planned to visit a local supermarket to buy supplies for them such as food, drink, some gifts and toys for the kids. The village is only accessible by boat, so we boarded a local water taxi and headed towards the village which took about 30 minutes.

We arrived at the village to an amazing welcome with the whole village on the shores to welcome us to their home. "Welcome, welcome, welcome they sang as we pulled in to the makeshift wooden jetty. I have to say I started to feel a little emotional as we pulled into the shore line. Seeing how happy they were to see us was wonderful. We were all greeted with high fives, hand shakes and introductions. A lot of the kids spoke very good English and were very well spoken. They took education very seriously.

We were taken to the village and shown around; all the children had a welcoming event for us where they sang songs for us. Once a week, Charles provides all the children a meal and today was the day. We watched as 200 hungry kids lined up in single file to receive a tiny portion of soup and bread. There was enough for a small portion each and no more, I never saw the adults eat anything and I remember children trying to come back for the second time and being turned away. There was just not enough food. This was quite a shock to me, think of the food waste we have in the UK. In this village, they would welcome what we throw away.

Once the children had eaten, they all slowly left to go home for the evening. Charles had started a bonfire for us, so we and the elders of the village sat around and got to know each other. We talked about life, family, how we can help, what they need and just had what a fantastic night was. We just chatted, nobody was on their phone, or iPad, just good old chat amongst friends and the crate of beer that Charles brought with him, made it even more fun.

The next day we woke up in the bush, and we planned to travel further into the village to see where else we could install a water facility. We traveled to the top of the village and found a site for the next tank and also one on the other side of the village. Seeing the effect that the first tank Samuel installed has made was awesome. The children were all healthy albeit hungry but they did not have to drink dirty river water anymore and that meant they were not getting infections and stomach bugs. It really had made a massive difference. Samuel deserves so much praise for his work in this village. If you want to see Charles and the village jump on YouTube, search

"Samuel Leeds Africa". You can see the first trip he made to this village.

We left the village and headed back to Entebbe as our trip was coming to an end. We had some stops planned on the way to assess new villages we can help. We identified a few more places which Samuel and his team are now in talks with the local planning offices to get the required permissions. Hopefully, these will be granted very soon.

What did I learn from my time in Uganda? Well firstly, don't go water rafting. No, seriously we in the UK have everything we need. We all need to think more about others and how we can help people less fortunate than us. I love what Samuel has done in Uganda and I hope to return there in 2019 to see the progress and find some more villages in need. I realised that life is precious and

you need to live it on your terms and not someone else's.
I loved Uganda and can't wait to return.

From Uganda I flew to Johannesburg, Samuel had
arranged for us to attend an event being hosted by Robert
Kiyosaki author of "Rich Dad, Poor Dad". Arguably one of
the top property investors in the world. His book is the first
investment book I read and it was great to be able to see
him in person. Samuel had also arranged for us to attend
a special dinner event with Robert and the other
speakers. This was a private event with around 25 other
guests and we all got time to chat with Robert and he held
an exclusive talk for around an hour detailing some of his
few known tactics and tax strategies.

The whole Africa trip was an absolute once in a lifetime experience, something I will never forget. I met some great people, made some lifelong friends and got to shake the hand of the guy whose book kicked off my investing journey.

So where are we now? As I finish off this book, I thought I'd lay out below what I have achieved. This is not to show off but merely show you that no matter where you are in your life, what doubts you have or what is holding you back that ANYONE can achieve the same and better results than I have. All you have to do is educate, implement and keep pushing every day.

**2018 Highlights**

o    Acquired 2 x 4-bed multi-let properties

o    Acquired an R2R Serviced accommodation property

o    Built Better Sourced Ltd from no income to sales of £30k per month and growing. Our projections will be hitting £35k per month within 3 months

o    Employed 2 x full-time members of staff for Better Sourced Ltd

o    Overcome my fear of speaking in front of a crowd. I regularly speak in front of audiences of 100 plus; biggest audience yet is 810

o    Started and hosted a Network Event "Property Investors Circle."

o    Built a large Investors Database

o    Have packaged and sold over 40 property deals

o      Have attended Rocky's Birthday party

There is more, but that should be enough to show you that no matter where you are now, a lot can happen in 12 months. For me, the most satisfying result I have had in the last 12 months is I am able to provide my wife with a job she enjoys. Lisa has never really enjoyed her work but did it because she had to. We are now in a position where Lisa can work in the business, and we can afford to pay her. She now works from home and only when the business needs her to. No more 9 – 5, no more having to pay a childminder and having to get up early to get everything done in time to get Isobel to the childminders and then get to work for 08:30.

I'm going to leave you with some action steps, so you can start straight away and I sincerely hope everyone reading this follows them

**Step 1.**

Educate, Educate, Educate.

Give yourself the gift of learning something you don't know. Please start educating yourself on property today. The best start would be to attend the Property Investors Crash Course by Samuel Leeds. You can get free tickets by emailing me at info@bettersourcedltd.co.uk or by visiting the website below. It's completely free to attend and you will learn loads, plus I'll be there and I can answer any questions you have.

www.property-investors.co.uk

**Step 2.**

Implement TODAY

Whether you attend an event, read a book or watch a YouTube video, you must learn to implement and put into action what you been taught. It is no use learning loads and doing nothing.

**Step 3.**

Ignore the doubters and little voices. Push on even if you are criticized. Push every day

**Step 4.**

Step out of your comfort zone. Do something every day that makes you feel uncomfortable. This could be something as simple as the next time you are on the train saying hello to the person sitting next to you. Get comfortable being uncomfortable

Whenever I get offered an opportunity, I say YES. I'll figure it out after.

**Step 5.**

Attend property networking events; they are very cheap to attend and you will meet many people just like you there. Network like crazy, remember add value to other people before you ask for something.

**Step 6.**

Get your finances in order so if you find a great deal you are prepared. Once you have assessed your financial position and spoken with a mortgage broker, decide which strategy would be the best suit your needs and finances. Once you decide on the strategy, learn as much as you can about it, Become a master on one strategy and not a jack of all.

**Step 7**.

Tune in every Friday at 4pm to the

"The Property Investors Podcast"

with myself and Russell Leeds

You can find it on YouTube, Spotify, apple podcast, audio-boom, apple podcast, and many other outlets. It a great way to get free information, help and hints.

**Step 8.**

Have fun, enjoy the journey and accept that you're going to come up against closed doors and struggles but believe if you can push past these, you will look back with no regrets.

**Step 9**.

Tell everyone what you're doing, you never know who among your circle of contacts may be looking for someone to joint venture with on a deal.

**Step 10.**

When you have any success, then celebrate. Let me know so I can celebrate with you especially if it is as a result of this book.

Thank you very much for getting to the end and I truly hope every single person who has made it here gets the result they deserve. Please take action and get out there.

I'd love to hear your thoughts on this book. If you found it useful, please share this with me and likewise let me know how it could be better.

*"Today I am no longer filled with self-doubt, negativity or a lack of self-confidence"*

# Keeping in touch

I'd love to hear of any success you get; I really hope I have inspired you to take action and step out. If you have enjoyed this book and found it helpful please let me know.

I can be contacted through the following channels

**WWW.ALASDAIR-CUNNINGHAM.COM**

**WWW.BETTERSOURCEDLTD.CO.UK**

Email – info@bettersourcedltd.co.uk

Phone – 07704 091 262

You can connect with me Facebook, Instagram and LinkedIn.

**PROPERTY INVESTORS PODCAST**

Search property investors podcast on YouTube

For media and speaking engagements, please contact **info@bettersourcedltd.co.uk**

# About the Author

Alasdair Cunningham is a normal family man who decided after 18 years grafting that there must be an easier way to earn an income. He sought out to find it and succeeded.

His wife Lisa has stood by his side through the ups and downs of his current and previous business which I believe deserves a medal. Lisa has always supported Alasdair even though at times thinks he was daft. They have 2 daughters Yazmin, who is a trainee conveyancer and Isobel who is in her first year of upper school and excels in mathematics.

Alasdair is the owner of Better Sourced Ltd and ALC Investment Properties Ltd.

He also runs the Property Investors Circle network event to get like-minded investors together monthly. Alasdair regularly gets invited to tell his story from stage to tell his story, considering that he would struggle to speak in front of a small audience a year ago just shows you how much he has grown in confidence and strength.

There have been many people who have helped me on my journey. I can't thank them enough but here goes;

**Lisa**, my ever-supportive wife, who has stood by me even when she hasn't agreed with what I am doing. I know I am hard work and thank you for all you support. Xx

**Samuel Leeds**, I Couldn't ask for a more devoted mentor and friend nothing has ever been too much trouble and you've always offered help, support and guidance. I will forever be grateful.

**Russell Leeds**, my podcast partner, I've really enjoyed getting to know you. Your support has been very much appreciated. You're a great friend and really great guy.

I can't thank the many friends I have met over the last 18 months enough, they have been there for me when I needed advice, a laugh or just a chat. In particular Paul and Ann Waters, Nick Mobley, John Raybould and Anna Leeds.

# What others say about

## Alasdair Cunningham.

*"Alasdair is a serious action taker, he knows what he wants and does whatever it takes to get there. With that being said he is certainly not a cut throat. He's a really nice, genuine and loyal guy, the sort of person who will always be there for you when you need him. I'm proud to call Alasdair a friend."*

Russel Leeds – CEO

*"With Alasdair's help, I purchased 4 x HMO properties, Alasdair was very open and honest throughout, and I'm pleased to say 16 out of the 18 rooms are now occupied and achieving a higher than expected income. I have no doubt the other rooms will fill very quickly- Great work Alasdair and I can't wait for the next deal."*

Michael – Expat 16 years in Hong Kong

*"I met Alasdair in September 2017 at a training event, my first thoughts were that he was a very genuine and nice person, a few things I picked up on were that he was quite cynical, sceptical, and full of self-doubt. Alasdair is a smart guy and I have witnessed Alasdair grow both as a*

*person and in business. He has become a lot more self-confident and started to believe in himself.*
*Congratulations on your success and personal growth"*

Stuart Brown – Finance Director